Contents

Introductory note — 2

Section one: Articles and letters by Joseph Hansen — 3

   1. The character of the new Cuban government — 3

   2. Nasser's Egypt—on the way to a workers state? — 7

   3. The Algerian revolution and the character of the Ben Bella regime — 23

   4. The social transformations in Eastern Europe, China, and Cuba — 29

   5. An exchange of letters between Joseph Hansen and Bob Chester — 39

Section two: Background materials on the 'workers and farmers government' — 53

   1. The workers government—Excerpts from the 'Theses on Tactics' and discussion at the Fourth World Congress of the Comintern — 53

   2. The call for a workers government in France — 62
      by Leon Trotsky

   3. From 'An Explanation in a Circle of Friends' — 64
      by Leon Trotsky

   4. From 'The Death Agony of Capitalism and the Tasks of the Fourth International' — 65

   5. On the slogan of 'workers and farmers government' — 67
      by Michel Pablo

   6. Report and discussion on the third Chinese revolution — 77
      May 1952 plenum of the Fourth International

   7. The Algerian revolution from 1962 to 1969 — 84
      1969 resolution of the Fourth International

Introductory note

In the revolutionary upsurge that followed World War II, capitalism was overturned in a number of countries (the Soviet-occupied zone of Eastern Europe, Yugoslavia, Albania, North Korea, China, and North Vietnam). Later the Cuban revolution also culminated in a socialist overturn.

All of these overturns shared a common feature—they were carried out by movements that were not headed by revolutionary-Marxist leaderships.

This fact appeared to fly in the face of the predictions made by such figures as Lenin and Trotsky that a Bolshevik-type party is required to bring down capitalism. Some difficult theoretical questions were thus raised for revolutionists. How could upheavals that were not headed by revolutionary Marxists end up in overturns that were socialist in principle? What was the nature of the process that made possible such an outcome? Could even antisocialist formations successfully substitute for revolutionary-Marxist leaderships throughout the world? Had the effort to build revolutionary-Marxist parties become outmoded?

One of the most active participants in the discussion on these questions in the world Trotskyist movement has been Joseph Hansen, a long-time leader of the Socialist Workers Party who is at present the editor of *Intercontinental Press,* a revolutionary-Marxist international newsweekly. Hansen suggested that the problem had already been adumbrated at the Fourth World Congress of the Communist International and that Trotsky had touched on it in the Transitional Program adopted by the Fourth International at its founding congress in 1938.

According to this view, the key link in the process by which a petty-bourgeois leadership, such as the one that headed the July 26 Movement in Cuba, can topple a capitalist government in exceptional circumstances is a "workers and peasants government."

Section One of this bulletin contains articles and letters by Hansen dealing with this concept and its exemplification. (Hansen's contribution to the discussion of the overturns in Eastern Europe can be found in the Education for Socialists bulletin, *Class, Party and State and the Eastern European Revolution.*)

In these writings, Hansen stresses the limitations of the process that led to the establishment of workers and peasants governments as a transitional step in countries like China and Cuba. He shows how, for instance, the weaknesses of the Ben Bella leadership in Algeria led to the overthrow of the workers and peasants government there.

Section Two of this collection contains background material on the origin and development of the concept of a workers and peasants government and examples of its application by the Fourth International in the cases of China and Algeria. Space considerations prevented the inclusion of some relevant material, notably Trotsky's explanation of the educational value of the demand for a workers and farmers government in the United States. This item appears in *The Transitional Program for Socialist Revolution* (New York: Pathfinder Press, first edition, 1973, third edition, 2014), pp. 252-53.

Fred Feldman

SECTION ONE: ARTICLES AND LETTERS BY JOSEPH HANSEN

1. The character of the new Cuban government

The following article by Joseph Hansen was written in July 1960 for consideration by the leadership of the Socialist Workers Party. Hansen held that the forced resignation of Manuel Urrutia as President of Cuba in July 1959 and the subsequent removal of Felipe Pazos as head of the National Bank (to be replaced by Che Guevara) marked the establishment of a workers and peasants government in Cuba. These shifts resulted from a sharp split between the bourgeois and the left wings of the Castro regime over the radical agrarian reform that had been initiated.

This analysis was adopted by the National Committee of the Socialist Workers Party in January 1961 in the "Draft Theses on the Cuban Revolution." These theses also concluded that Cuba had become a workers state through the sweeping nationalizations carried out in the fall of 1960.

The same conclusion was reached almost simultaneously by the wing of the world Trotskyist movement that adhered to the International Secretariat. A congress of this group held in January 1961 approved a resolution stating that "Cuba has ceased to be a capitalist state, and is becoming a workers' state through the application of the nationalization measures of October 1960." Agreement on this important point speeded the reunification of the Fourth International that took place in 1963.

The Cuban revolution has proved to be deep-going. Beginning with the simple political objective of overthrowing Batista's army-police dictatorship, it rapidly disclosed its tendency to revolutionize economic and social relations and to extend its influence throughout Latin America and beyond.

The main force opposing the logical development of the Cuban revolution is American imperialism. But the measures it has taken in attempting to stem the revolution and eventually suffocate it have had the opposite effect of spurring it forward.

The new Cuban government that took power in January 1959 has played a positive role up to now in the development of the revolution. First it secured its governing position by smashing the old armed forces and the police. It supplanted these with the rebel army, a new police largely recruited from the ranks of the revolutionary fighters, and later it set up a people's militia almost entirely proletarian and peasant in composition. It rapidly undertook a radical agrarian reform. This has two forms: (1) division of the land among the peasants on a limited private ownership basis (the land cannot be sold or mortgaged); (2) co-operatives closely tied to government planning. The emphasis has been on the side of the co-operatives. By last fall the government initiated planning of industry and control of foreign trade. A new stage was opened with the expropriation of land held by the sugar interests. Most recently, under the pressure of American imperialism, measures of expropriation have been extended to important foreign industrial holdings (principally American) and a virtual monopoly of foreign trade has been instituted.

A significant indication of the direction of movement of the Castro government is its tendency to establish friendly relations not only with the so-called "neutral" powers but with the Soviet bloc. This includes trade pacts that cut across the long-established trade pattern with the U.S. More important, however, is the tendency to emulate the planned economic structure of the Soviet countries.

The Castro government has proved that its responses to the mass revolutionary movement in Cuba and to the counterpressure from the U.S. are not simply passive. The new government has courageously defied American imperialism, resisting blandishments, threats and reprisals. On the domestic side, it has repeatedly mobilized the Cuban workers and peasants in political demonstrations, in taking over landlord and capitalist holdings, in disarming the forces of the old regime and in arming the people.

The direction of development on the political side has been demonstrated in the series of crises surmounted by the government since it took power. At first it put bourgeois democratic figures in key positions (finances, foreign trade, diplomacy, even the presidency). With each crisis induced by the interaction of imperialist and revolutionary pressures, these figures either turned against the government or were pushed out, being replaced by active participants in the preceding civil war, however youthful and inexperienced in their new duties.

The bourgeois outposts in such fields as the press, radio and TV have suffered a parallel liquidation. On the other hand, workers and peasant organizations, including political tendencies, have been granted freedom of expression on the one condition that they support the revolutionary measures taken by the new government.

The Castro leadership began in 1952–53 as a radical petty-bourgeois movement, but one that took its revolutionary language seriously. It organized and led an insurrection. In power it sought (a) to bring the various revolutionary tendencies together in a common front by giving them due representation in government offices and by opposing any witch-hunting, (b) to form a coalition with the remnants of the bourgeois-democratic movements that had survived the Batista dictatorship. The coalition, in which these elements were a minority unable to set policy, proved to be unstable. The defection of Miro Cardona a few weeks after being appointed ambassador to the United States epitomized the instability of the coalition at the same time that it appears to have marked its end.

The Castro leadership has shown awareness of its own origin and its own leftward evolution, including the stages through which it has developed. What is remarkable is its acceptance of this development and its repeated declarations to follow through to the end, "no matter what," and despite its own surprise at the turns that open up. The constantly emphasized concept of the Cuban revolution as an "example" for Latin America, as the first link in a new chain of revolutions in Latin America against Wall Street's domination, is especially to be noted as an indication of awareness that the leadership of the Cuban revolution faces great historic responsibilities.

The dynamic rather than static character of the Castro leadership, of extraordinary interest to the revolutionary-socialist movement, is undoubtedly ascribable in large part to the world setting in which the Cuban revolution occurs. It has the examples of the Soviet Union, China and Yugoslavia as well as the examples of colonial insurgency in a series of countries. These examples, plus the material aid and moral encouragement to be obtained from such sources, plus the feeling of participating in a worldwide revolutionary upsurge, have had a powerful effect on the outlook of the Castro leadership.

In addition, this leadership is close to the mass movement of both the peasants and workers, who have solidly and militantly supported each revolutionary measure and inspired their leaders to go further. The popular response throughout Latin America has had a further effect in the same direction.

All this points to the conclusion that the new Cuban government is a "Workers and Farmers Government" of the kind defined in our Transitional Program as "a government independent of the bourgeoisie."

This does not signify that a workers state has been established in Cuba. What has been established is a highly contradictory and highly unstable regime, subject to pressures and impulses that can move it forward or backward. Enjoying the support of the workers and peasants, having led them in a political revolution, faced with the imperative need to carry the revolution forward to its culmination by toppling bourgeois economic and social relations and extending the revolution throughout Latin America and into the United States, the regime lacks the socialist consciousness (program) to accomplish this. Even if it carries out extensive expropriations, these, precisely because of the lack of socialist consciousness, are not so assured as to be considered a permanent foundation of the state. In its bourgeois consciousness, the regime falls short of the objective needs of the revolution. (Whether the decay of capitalism and the example and influence of planned economies elsewhere in the world can make up for this lack—and to what extent—need not concern us here.)

Insofar as such a government takes practical measures against the bourgeoisie; that is, begins to resolve its contradictory position in the direction of socialism, it warrants support. And insofar as it grants democratic rights to revolutionary socialism, it warrants a fraternal attitude. Against imperialism, it must, of course, be supported unconditionally.

Whether the Castro regime, or a section of it will evolve until it achieves socialist consciousness remains to be seen. As a petty-bourgeois formation it can retrogress. Its direction of evolution, however, has certainly been encouraging up to now.

By recognizing the new Cuban government as a "Workers and Farmers Government," we indicate its radical petty-bourgeois background and composition and its origin in a popular mass movement, its tendency to respond to popular pressures for action against the bourgeoisie and their agents, and its capacity, for whatever immediate reasons and with whatever hesitancy, to undertake measures against bourgeois political power and against bourgeois property relations. The extent of these measures is not decisive in determining the nature of the regime. What is decisive is the capacity and the tendency.

The Fourth Congress discussion
The concept "Workers and Farmers Government" is not at all a new one. At the Fourth Congress of the Comintern in 1922, it was discussed at some length. In view of the encouraging prospects then facing the Third International and the known characteristics of such formations as the Mensheviks, the possibility was not considered great that a petty-bourgeois government in opposition to the bourgeoisie would actually appear. But it was considered a possibility and some of its characteristics were delineated. These offer us criteria by which to measure the new Cuban government. For instance, the "Theses on Tactics" declares:

The overriding tasks of the workers' government must be to arm the proletariat, to disarm bourgeois counterrevolutionary organizations, to introduce the control of production, to transfer the main burden of taxation to the rich, and to break the resistance of the counterrevolutionary bourgeoisie. [See Section 2 of this collection for a new translation of this item.]

The document continues by declaring that "Such a workers' government is only possible if it is born out of the struggle of the masses, is supported by workers' bodies which are capable of fighting, bodies created by the most oppressed sections of the working masses."

The new Cuban government has obviously met these criteria, even if we include an item not stated by the authors of the "Theses": the task of "resolutely opposing imperialist rule."

It is true that the Bolsheviks had before them the petty-bourgeois organizations of their time and not a government formed by something as revolutionary-minded as the July 26 Movement; but then in discussing possible forms of a "Workers and Farmers Government" they left room for variants which they could not predict and which it was fruitless to speculate about.

The main value to be derived from thus classifying the new Cuban government is not simply to be able to use a correct designation but in the possibility it opens—from the viewpoint of consistent theory—to apply the politics suggested by the Fourth Congress and by our Transitional Program in relation to such governments.

Trotsky's position in 1938
Trotsky was one of the guiding, if not the chief guiding spirit at the Fourth Congress in 1922. He considered its main documents, like those of the previous three congresses, as part of the programmatic foundation of the Fourth International. He clearly had the discussion at the Fourth Congress in mind when he wrote the section on "Workers and Farmers Government" in the Transitional Program in 1938. This section, consequently, becomes much richer in content and implication if the previous discussion in 1922 is borne in mind.

Trotsky repeats one of the main points—that one of the uses of the formula of "Workers and Farmers Government" was as a pseudonym for the dictatorship of the proletariat, first in the agitation of the Bolsheviks in preparing to take power, later as a popular designation for the proletarian dictatorship that was established. Trotsky emphasizes this in order to contrast what Stalinism did with the pseudonym after usurping power. Comparing what Trotsky says with the declarations of the "Theses on Tactics" adopted at the Fourth Congress, we see that Stalinism supported those types of "workers" governments opposed by the Bolsheviks as masked forms of bourgeois power. In this way, Trotsky brings the "Theses on Tactics" up to date on this point by including the historic experience with Stalinism in relation to the concept of "Workers and Farmers Government."

As for a different use of the formula "Workers and Farmers Government"—the one that concerns us here—to designate a regime that is neither bourgeois nor proletarian but something in between, he generalizes the entire experience since 1917 in an exceedingly condensed sentence: "The experience of Russia demonstrated and the experience of Spain and France once again confirms that even under very favorable conditions the parties of the petty-bourgeois democracy (S.R.'s, Social-Democrats, Stalinists, Anarchists) are incapable of creating a government of workers and peasants, that is, a government independent of the bourgeoisie."

This appears to rule out the "possibility," discussed at the Fourth Congress, of the actual formation of such governments. However, Trotsky refused to make an absolute out of his generalization of some twenty years of historic experience. Instead he affirms the position of the Fourth Congress in the following well-known paragraph:

> Is the creation of such a government by the traditional workers organizations possible? Past experience shows, as has already been stated, that this is to say the least highly improbable. However, one cannot categorically deny in advance the theoretical possibility that, under the influence of completely exceptional circumstances (war, defeat, financial crash, mass revolutionary pressure, etc.) the petty-bourgeois parties, including the Sta-

linists, may go further than they themselves wish along the road to a break with the bourgeoisie. In any case one thing is not to be doubted: even if this highly improbable variant somewhere at some time becomes a reality and the 'Workers and Farmers Government,' in the above-mentioned sense, is established in fact, it would represent merely a short episode on the road to the actual dictatorship of the proletariat.

In explaining the political value of the formula as a slogan, aside from the question of its actual historical realization, Trotsky stands on the position of the Fourth Congress: (1) It is an extremely important weapon for exposing the treacherous character of the old petty-bourgeois leaderships. (2) It has tremendous educational value, for it "proceeds entirely along the line of the political development of our epoch (the bankruptcy and decomposition of the old petty-bourgeois parties, the downfall of democracy, the growth of fascism, the accelerated drive of the workers toward more active and aggressive politics)."

Trotsky does no more than suggest the historic conditions that might convert the possibility of a Workers and Farmers Government ("a government independent of the bourgeoisie") from something "highly improbable" into something quite probable and even into a reality. Some twenty years later we can see that the main historic conditions turned out to be the continued crisis in the leadership of the proletariat (the long default, due to Stalinism, in taking advantage of revolutionary opportunities) coupled with the continued decay of capitalism and the mounting pressure of popular movements seeking a way out, plus the survival of the Soviet Union in World War II and the subsequent strengthening of its world position.

Trotsky did not deal with the tactical problems that would face our movement should such a government actually be formed. The reasons for this are clear enough: (1) On the eve of World War II the possibility of such a government actually appearing was remote. (2) The basic strategy from which to derive tactics was well known, involving no more than the application of the Leninist attitude toward petty-bourgeois formations in the two possible variants of their development—

toward or away from Marxism. (3) The Fourth Congress in its "Theses on Tactics" had already specified the conditions under which such a government would be supported or opposed. (4) The main issues confronting such a possible government would be the same in general as those for which key transitional slogans were proposed; these could be modified to fit whatever specific case might arise.

In conclusion, whatever the particular circumstances were that gave rise to a government of the type now seen in Cuba, the possibility of the appearance of such a government was foreseen long ago by the Bolsheviks, its relation to the world revolutionary process was anticipated, and a general concept of how to approach it was worked out even down to specific slogans. In the abstract form of a transitional slogan we are, in fact, thoroughly familiar with it.

Its appearance in the form of a living reality does not overthrow our theory. On the contrary, the actual appearance of a government like the one in Cuba would seem to offer a most brilliant confirmation of the lucidity of Marxist thought and its power to forecast. It would also seem to constitute the most heartening evidence of the grand possibilities now opening up for revolutionary socialism and the party that has kept its theoretical heritage alive.

Joseph Hansen
JULY 1960

2. Nasser's Egypt—on the way to a workers state?

The discussion of the post–World War Two social transformations has continued to have theoretical repercussions in the Trotskyist movement. In 1965, prior to the Second World Congress since reunification of the Fourth International, Livio Maitan, a leader of the Italian Trotskyists, proposed the hypothesis that countries like Egypt, which had carried out extensive nationalizations under petty-bourgeois nationalist leadership could possibly become workers states in time without a mass revolutionary uprising. In answering this view, Joseph Hansen wrote the following article, first published in the December 1965 *International Information Bulletin*, published by the SWP as a fraternal courtesy to the United Secretariat of the Fourth International.

In his contribution, "Some Criticisms and Comments Concerning the Document on the African Revolution," Comrade Livio Maitan advances the hypothesis that in certain countries like Nasser's Egypt, it may be possible for a workers state to emerge in a "relatively cold way, without the active revolutionary intervention of the masses at the crucial moment of the qualitative leap."

From the form of his contribution—a detailed presentation of the original and amended paragraphs of the document submitted by the United Secretariat for discussion in the Fourth International *(Theses on the Progress and Problems of the African Revolution)*—the impression could be gained that serious differences have appeared in the United Secretariat over the assessment of the situation and tasks in Africa. However, Comrade Maitan himself assures us that although his hypothesis was rejected, the highest body of the world Trotskyist movement, of which he is a member, is in complete agreement on the "general line of the document, on the class nature of a number of African states at the present stage, on the tasks of the revolutionary Marxists. . . ."

The differences would thus appear to be part of the normal process of democratically determining a general line, in which one-sided, tentative, or dubious items are sifted out in favor of more correct and precise approximations. This process of collective thought is not yet finished in the development of the document under discussion; and one may expect additional changes to be made in the theses before they are finally adopted at the coming world congress of the Fourth International.[1] By the seriousness with which it carries out this process, the Fourth International gives proof of its internal democracy. The world Trotskyist movement differs considerably from organizations where the texts prepared by the leaders are offered for mere ratification by the rank and file.

Comrade Maitan, in fact, argues only for leaving open what he considers to be a theoretical possibility—one that has occurred nowhere up to now, as he himself indicates. Thus he does not disagree with the other comrades of the United Secretariat on how to characterize the *present* reality and the *present* tasks of revolutionary Marxists in Africa or anywhere else.

From this, I would conclude that the United Secretariat made a correct decision in taking the course it did. The reasons for the amendments can be deduced by reading the sections of the original rough draft drawn up by Comrade Maitan, which he quotes, and comparing them with the modifications agreed upon by the body as a whole. The changes of substance involve almost exclusively his hypothesis. On the one hand, a speculative idea was taken out of a resolution outlining current tasks and demanding the widest possible agreement consistent with basic principles. On the other hand, by separating a difference of this kind from the general line—on which the United Secretariat, be it repeated, is unanimous—conditions were enhanced for a free and fruitful discussion of the hypothesis on its own merits.

After these preliminaries, intended to indicate the frame of discussion, let us turn to the question itself.

First of all, it must be noted that the discussion is not a matter of doctrinal hair-splitting—a complex real world confronts us and we have no choice as Marxists but to seek to give it correct reflection in theory so as to provide a firm basis for action. The truth is that some quite spectacular measures have been passed in a series of countries which cannot be dismissed with simple generalizations. A good summary of developments in Egypt can be found in Hassan Riad's informative *L'Egypte Nassérienne*,[2] from which we offer the following:

Sweeping nationalizations

At the end of this evolution, in 1963, the Egyptian economy had thus been almost completely nationalized . . . at least in its modern sectors. The banks, the insurance companies, transport, the mines and basic industries, foreign trade—are, save for rare exceptions, statized; almost all the big concerns in light industry (textiles, agricultural and food industries, etc.), wholesale trade and the big stores are under a mixed economy. The formal conditions—the abolition of the private property of big capital—have thus been fulfilled for the socialist transformation of Egyptian society. If some vestiges of private property still officially remain, it cannot be held that maintenance of a sector of mixed economy, in an underdeveloped country, proves that the dominant character of the economic system is capitalist. Moreover, even in this mixed sector, the powers of the state are considerable—the state names by decree the company management boards, and the national offices keep close watch over them.

The 1961 laws very seriously limited the domain and powers of big private capital. It has already been mentioned that the law sets a maximum of 10,000 pounds [$22,700] which an individual can own in stocks. In addition, the rate of the progressive income tax reaches 90% on everything above 15,000 pounds [$34,050] a year. This measure does not affect a good part of the bureaucracy whose incomes are relatively modest, at least so far as legal incomes are concerned; but it unquestionably affects big private capital.

---

1. For instance, Comrade Maitan calls attention to an overstatement in one of the amendments to his original rough draft: "As yet, history has not furnished us with an example of any country achieving this [the qualitative leap to a workers state] without a deep-going popular revolution." It is evident that it would be more accurate in this statement to indicate the historic exception of military conquest at the hands of a workers state, as happened in Eastern Europe. We will return to this point later.

2. *L'Egypte Nasserienne* by Hassan Riad. Editions de Minuit, 7 rue Bernard-Palissy, Paris 6, 1964, 252 pp. 13,50 francs. In quoting from this study, we have provided our own translations.

> The evolution which began in 1953 with the creation of the Council for Production, and which reached a serious take-off point in 1957 with the nationalization of French-British capital has now almost been completed with the laws of 1961. Moreover, nothing shows that the regime will not go still further, that it will not liquidate the last vestiges of the private property of big capital, that it will not simply undertake outright nationalization of the companies in the mixed economy. (pp. 222–223)

The sweeping nationalizations in Egypt, placing the state in charge of the financial and credit system, the basic industries and trade, offer a real problem in classification. Exactly what is the correct label for the Egypt of today?

The Nasser government claims that Egypt has become a "socialist" country and many observers agree with this. Thus Hassan Riad continues his comments:

> This impressive evolution, the liquidation of the former bourgeois aristocracy, gave the impression that Nasserism would open the road to the progressive construction of a socialist society. This is, moreover, what Cairo's official propaganda claims. In accordance with this, the agrarian reform was to liquidate the 'feudal regime' in the countryside; convert rural society into a society of small proprietors; and, by organizing them into cooperatives, open up the road to a socialist evolution. The development of the economy, nationalized to an extent almost comparable to that of the Communist countries, would, within the framework of a plan, permit Egypt's historic backwardness to be liquidated, thus preparing the conditions for an out-and-out socialist society. Political figures, journalists, foreign tourists, taken to visit the ultramodern Kafreldawar textile plants, the Helwan steel mills, the construction sites of the High Dam, depart, convinced of the immense effort, persuaded that the Nasserite regime has done as much as the other socialist regimes that have gone through the same phase, that of accelerated accumulation of capital in a backward country. The reservations which they express concerning the police regime, the religious fanaticism, does not lessen their conviction that despite everything the Nasserite regime can pride itself on major socialist accomplishments. (p. 223)

The Egyptian Communist party also came to this conclusion and decided that it would be logical to dissolve, the better to support Nasser. As its dying act, the central committee issued a declaration last April, hailing the "socialist policy of Nasser" and stating that Nasser's party, the Arab Socialist Union, is capable of carrying out all the tasks of constructing socialism.

Another current of opinion, seeking to give better balance to the combination of authoritarianism represented by the Nasser regime and what appear to be measures of a socialist nature, at least in form, holds that Egypt must be characterized as a deformed workers state.

The problem of the qualitative leap

These two positions are, in the final analysis, based on a single criterion—that nationalizations in and of themselves, if extensive enough, make the state "socialist" or at least proletarian in character. Since very extensive nationalizations have occurred in Egypt, it thus follows, according to this line of thinking, that Egypt must be some kind of "socialist" or "workers" state.

If we were to ask those who hold either of these positions why it should be concluded that nationalizations per se are socialist or proletarian by nature, we would probably not get a very clear answer. Probably they would say that if 10% of industry is nationalized, that's not socialist. After all, in many countries the post office and even the railways are run by the government and that doesn't mean we are dealing with a workers state. But 75%! That's something different. . . . And what's qualitatively different? Well, that's hard to say, but would a *capitalist* state go as far as that?

Very likely an effort to determine if there are any other reasons except the extensive nationalizations that would require us to call Egypt a "socialist" or "workers" state "as of now" would not be of much interest to these analysts. For them the mere quantity of nationalizations is enough.

Fortunately, Comrade Maitan does not belong to this school. He agrees that Egypt as of now is neither a "socialist" nor a "workers" state. He is therefore not confronted with the problem of stating why nationalizations in and of themselves should automatically be held to be "socialist" or "proletarian" no matter what the related circumstances.

Unfortunately, for his hypothesis, however, this does not strengthen its claim to validity. His position is, we recall, that it is not excluded that "in the present Egyptian context, even the bureaucratic layer, subjected only to the pressure of the status quo and its own interests, under very specific given conditions, can be pushed to adopt outright anticapitalist measures." We ask with some curiosity, "Exactly what 'outright anticapitalist measures' does Comrade Maitan have in mind?"

Obviously he is not thinking of nationalizations alone, or he would consider Egypt to be a workers state "as of now." Perhaps he envisages a sweeping change in the ideology of the layer now governing Egypt which would then be concretized in action? This is suggested by a sentence such as: "In this case leaderships of petty-bourgeois and revolutionary-democratic formation would be more and more inspired by the historic demands proper to the working class and of the socialist movement; and from this fact the social content of their action would change qualitatively."

But this stands in contradiction to the concept that "even the bureaucratic layer" in Egypt, "subjected only to the pressure of the status quo and its own interests"—without any special inspiration—could achieve the change. Comrade Maitan emphasizes this by asserting that in his opinion ". . . if the process, widely begun, should develop in a consistent fashion, *no matter what the intentions of the leaders*, it would end in the elimination of capitalist relations and the introduction of collectivist relations, characteristic of a workers state." (Emphasis added.) Moreover, when Comrade Maitan argues that: "leaderships of petty-bourgeois and revolutionary-democratic formation" can become inspired by historic demands proper to the working class and the socialist movement, he is evidently thinking of formations like the movement headed by Fidel Castro in its early phases. Is it really possible to visualize "special circumstances" that might inspire the present bureaucratic layer in Egypt to raise the banner of revolutionary Marxism? The probability for such a miracle is zero.

Finally, if this calculation of the mathematical probabilities turns out to be wrong, what would be the decisive criterion for testing the appearance of a genuinely socialist outlook in the Nasserite group—or a sector of it? Nothing less than mobilizing the active revolutionary intervention of the masses in the example set by Fidel Castro! But then this is not what Comrade Maitan has in mind. He visualizes a "qualitative leap" without the involvement of the masses.

The nature of this qualitative leap thus remains quite obscure. Yet it is absolutely decisive to the validity of the hypothesis. It involves nothing less than the one or more criterions which Comrade Maitan considers to be essential in determining the nature of a workers state, deformed or otherwise.

It may appear strange that we should ask Comrade Maitan for specifications on the content of "outright anticapitalist measures"; surely the nature of these are well enough known among revolutionary Marxists! It must be agreed that ordinarily we take elementary things for granted and do not ask that they be repeated over and over as in a kindergarten or in a group of ultraleft sectarians who can never get past the ABC's. In this case, however, Comrade Maitan's hypothesis concerns a basic matter—the criteria for determining a workers state. He introduces something new, the concept of a "cold" process and this at once raises a series of fundamental questions. Comrade Maitan himself had to refer to these in his contribution to the discussion; and, of course, they are explicitly involved in the theses on the African revolution. Thus to insist on this point is quite in order.

The absence of specifications on the nature of the "qualitative leap," as advanced in Comrade Maitan's hypothesis, is not at all compensated for by arguments attacking the essential nature of the criterions included in the theses on the African revolution submitted for discussion by the United Secretariat.

A minor example is Comrade Maitan's criticism of the criterion included by the United Secretariat as a test in determining the class nature of the present Egyptian state: "The state structure inherited from the former regime remains largely intact."

Against this, Comrade Maitan recalls "antecedents, where the birth of a workers state went along, at least for a certain period, with the maintenance of the former state structures." This is accurate. The state headed by Lenin and Trotsky in 1917 was called a workers state before the old administration had been smashed and the capitalist economy overturned. However, the recognition that a workers state had been born in October 1917 was based on the program of the Bolsheviks and political confidence in the will and integrity of the Bolsheviks to carry it out. A comparable situation can hardly be said to exist in Nasser's Egypt. It is difficult therefore to understand the relevancy of Comrade Maitan's observation. His contribution to the discussion clearly shows that he would place no political confidence in Nasser, even in the strictly hypothetical case of his unconsciously fathering a deformed workers state.

It should be added that in Eastern Europe, China, and in Cuba, the world Trotskyist movement did not recognize the existence of a workers state until the old state structure had actually been smashed. The reservations of the Trotskyists were due to their lack of political confidence in the leaderships in these countries, a consequence either of their record (the Kremlin) or their stated programs (China and Cuba). There is no good reason whatsoever for discarding this criterion in the case of Egypt, Mali, etc., at least so far as the present ruling layer is concerned.

The case of Eastern Europe

Let us turn to Comrade Maitan's objection to including "a deep-going popular revolution" as a criterion in determining the birth of a workers state. The difference over this point is quite important.

I would say that outside of a case of military conquest, this criterion is essential in determining whether or not a workers state has been born. A workers state is based not only on nationalizations but, among other things, on the revolutionary consciousness of the masses, a reciprocal of the revolutionary consciousness of the leadership. The great school for the masses in achieving this level is a popular revolution—a profound collective experience in mobilizing against the ruling class and its system in order to put an end to it and to consciously open up new historic possibilities. In judging a workers state as a whole, the degree of consciousness of the masses must be taken into account as one of the decisive items. (Comrade Maitan objects to this. However, the socialist consciousness of the masses has been of key importance in maintaining the Soviet Union as a workers state and was so regarded by Trotsky.)

Comrade Maitan's hypothesis is that Egypt—and not only Egypt—can become a workers state without such a popular revolution. As an argument he points to the case of Eastern Europe following World War II, where he contends, "the factor of 'intervention' by or 'pressure' of the masses did not play a greater role than in Egypt."

Since this analogy is closely connected with Comrade Maitan's strongest argument, it is important to understand it. I will begin by noting the dubiousness of the analogy. When Eastern Europe was occupied by Soviet troops, the big question was what the fate of the countries there would reveal about the character of the Soviet Union after the many years of Stalinist degeneration. If they remained capitalist in structure and continued under Soviet occupation, this could signify a rapid end for the Soviet Union as a workers state. When the Kremlin finally undertook the series of anti-capitalist measures that converted the countries of Eastern Europe into deformed workers states, this proved, as the Trotskyist movement said at the time, that the embers of the October revolution were still alive. Eastern Europe was converted into a "glacis"—an outer slope of the Soviet fortress. This was the primary significance of the overturns there. They testified that the Soviet Union was still a workers state.

The conversions were carried out by bureaucratic military means under the direct control of the bureaucracy standing on the Soviet property forms inherited from the October Revolution, dilapidated though they had become under Stalin's dictatorial rule. Even then, it is not altogether accurate to ascribe the initiative in the process to the Soviet bureaucracy.

As the Soviet armies defeated the German imperialist troops and swept into the countries that had suffered terrible years of Nazi occupation, native fascist regimes and the horrors of the Second World War, they were greeted with an enthusiasm that reached the proportions of popular uprisings in some cities. There could be not the slightest mistake concerning the revolutionary socialist import of the jubilation of the masses in Eastern Europe over the Soviet victory. This was particularly clear to Stalin. He sought to bottle up this elemental force with its dangerous meaning for his own rule. Some sectors of the Soviet troops gave the masses of Eastern Europe their first direct taste of the bitter meaning of Stalinism. This was followed by plundering and stripping the countries, even entire factories being carted away.

At first Stalin's policy was to maintain capitalism in Eastern Europe against the will of the masses. This was one of his great crimes, for if the Kremlin had responded to the initiative of the masses in Eastern Europe, the advance of the revolution there would have dovetailed with the popular uprisings in Western Europe and the whole continent would have gone socialist as early as 1947.

Nor were the masses entirely missing when Stalin finally did issue the order to go ahead with the overturn of capitalism in Eastern Europe as a reply to Churchill's and Truman's initiation of the cold war. Stalin had to rely in part on native leaders of the masses in these countries. This phase was then followed by the liquidation of these potential "Titoists" or "Trotskyists" in a series of frame-up trials—further evidence in its way of the "dangerous" socialist consciousness of the masses.

It was still not possible abroad, however, to be absolutely sure that this consciousness had not been destroyed by Stalinism until decisive confirmation of its continued existence was provided by the Hungarian uprising in 1956, when the masses in a spontaneous uprising themselves organized revolutionary councils which placed the preservation of nationalized, planned economy at the top of the slogans of the political revolution. This popular upsurge was so mighty that only Khrushchev's tanks, cheered on by Mao, could put it down.

What does this analogy tell us about Egypt? Not a great deal, it would seem—unless Comrade Maitan visualizes that Egypt might be occupied by Soviet armies under the command of a Soviet bureaucracy still guided by policies of the kind followed by Stalin immediately following World War II. Is this very likely?

But in order to preserve the analogy for the sake of argument, let us concede that such a remotely possible event is not absolutely excluded, even in a world coming ever closer to nuclear war. What happens then to the hypothesis on the possible revolutionary role that might be played by the "bureaucratic layer" in Egypt? And "through the play of factors that have operated up to now"? And "no matter what the intentions of the leaders"?

'Weakness' as a point of origin

Of course, Comrade Maitan may respond that all of this is ridiculous. He is perfectly familiar with the role played by the Kremlin and Soviet armed force in the conversion of Eastern Europe into deformed workers states. His point did not deal with that. The analogy he was drawing was between the weakness of the old structures in Eastern Europe and those in the countries in question today: "The substantial side in Eastern Europe was that the national bourgeoisie was so feeble, the old structures so broken up, the possibilities of intervention by imperialism so meager that bureaucratic-military means without the revolutionary intervention of the masses proved sufficient to overturn capitalism. In the countries in question today, it is essentially on the evidence of the extreme weakness of the conservative forces both national and international—that I base the hypothesis of formation, for example, of a workers state in Egypt in a relatively cold way, without the active revolutionary intervention of the masses at the crucial moment of the qualitative leap."

Comrade Maitan's hypothesis is obviously based on very abstract considerations. The conservative forces were weak in Eastern Europe; a workers state was born there. The conservative forces are weak today in a whole series of countries; therefore . . .

But Marxist theory is concrete. The weak feudal-capitalist structure in Eastern Europe went down under the combined blows of war, mass revulsion to the war, mass support for a Soviet victory, a mass upsurge with the arrival of the Soviet armies, the rise of indigenous revolutionary leaderships, a decision by the Kremlin (a very real power) to go ahead—all this, plus the application of bureaucratic-military means.

Let us advance a step further. A series of workers states, beginning with Yugoslavia, have appeared in a different way. In all of them, popular revolution acted as the decisive power that toppled the old structures—none of which proved to be very solid in face of a profound mass upsurge.

In both Eastern Europe and in all the subsequent overturns, up to the most recent one in Cuba, the weakness of the conservative forces was *relative* to the opposing forces. In Eastern Europe a shattered native capitalist structure and an imperialism weakened by mass revolts in Europe and the "Get Us Home" movement of the American troops, collided with Soviet power freshly victorious over German imperialism. In the other overturns, the old structures were overwhelmed by mobilized, insurgent masses, the mightiest power on earth.

Comrade Maitan's hypothesis advances something new; namely, the possibility of workers states now appearing in a series of countries without either the direct military intervention of a power like the Soviet Union or the power of popular revolution bringing the masses in strength onto the political scene. Comrade Maitan's hypothesis is that a petty-bourgeois formation can substitute for both of these powers.

It is to be noted that this reasoning places the petty bourgeois formation a priori on the side of progress, automatically against the weak conservative forces; and this regardless of whether the petty bourgeois formation is itself conservative-minded. The assumption of the automatic progressiveness of such formations, however, remains to be proved. Up to now, as Comrade Maitan agrees, little evidence can be found for it. To cite from a 1960 document evaluating the bonapartism of the ruling layer in countries of Black Africa can scarcely substitute for hard facts. The evaluation may have been in error or Comrade Maitan may be drawing unwarranted implications from it. The truth is that the hypothesis remains in the realm of speculation.

By gradual steps?

One of Comrade Maitan's concepts is only adumbrated. This is the idea that a workers state can be achieved through a "cold process"; i.e., through gradual steps that "end in the elimination of capitalist relations and the introduction of collectivist relations, characteristic of a workers state."

What Comrade Maitan means precisely is far from clear. The gates seem open to all kinds of surmises. Since the revolutionary mobilization of the masses is not required, according to this hypothesis, does "cold process" include the idea of achieving a workers state, deformed though it would be—by peaceful means? What are the possibilities that must be left open on this to fit in with the hypothesis?

We note, in passing, that Nasser is not exactly peaceful in his attitude toward the proletariat and the peasantry. "The evolution towards 'socialism' must proceed without a class struggle," says Anouar Abdel-Malek, describing Nasserism in his book *Egypte Société Militaire*. "The organs of struggle of the working class and the fellahs are abruptly dismantled—no communist party, no trade unions built and led by the workers themselves. The left is invited to dissolve itself into the single party, by way of the concentration camps; and the dissolved unions are reconstituted by the state in the form of a single union for each trade or profession, their leaders chosen and named by the apparatus, their essential field conceived to be primarily that of providing the regime with masses to be manipulated against imperialism, not directed against the class in power. From the beginning, the agrarian reform, instituted from above, aimed at neutralizing direct action by the fellahs." (p. 364)

It is true, of course, that parallels can be found in Stalinist practice; and repressive measures of this kind would not necessarily deny a country the label of "workers state"—a "degenerated" or "deformed" workers state, it is understood. But in the absence of the political criteria associated with the appearance of a democratic proletarian power, the economic and sociological criteria become all the more important, and along with it the question of the qualitative leap.

As the ultimate generator of the hypothetical "cold process," Comrade Maitan appears to have in mind not so much the "intrinsic forces and dynamics" of the indigenous petty bourgeois formations as the "historic world context." If we grasp the idea correctly the state bureaucracy headed by Nasser, for instance, could hypothetically serve as a transmission belt in a process having as its end result "a consistent evolution toward collectivist structures." The power source is a dual one: on the one hand, the weakness of imperialism and its bad examples; on the other, the rising strength of the workers states and the inspiration of their achievements.

I would be the last to deny the increasing repercussions of the mounting contrast between the two systems. It has become a very powerful factor in world politics and will inevitably increase in importance. It is undeniable, too, that indigenous ruling circles in many parts of the world have been affected by it in addition to the masses, although in a different way. Besides seeking to play the two camps against each other, the rulers of the "neutralist" countries, for instance, tend to bow in the Soviet direction by instituting "plans" and making liberal use of the "socialist" label.

It is something else again to visualize this process as so omnipotent that the apparatus of a capitalist state, like the one headed by Nasser, might gradually increase its imitation of Soviet institutions until the masses wake up one morning and see that somehow or other their country has been converted by its rulers to collectivist structures.

The hypothesis is similar to the hypothesis of "convergence." According to this theory, the Soviet Union is gradually, in an evolutionary way, taking on many of the "good" characteristics of Western capitalism, such as its alleged appreciation of "human" values, while Western capitalism is meanwhile gradually, in an evolutionary way, taking on some of the "good" characteristics of the Soviet Union, such as "economic planning." Eventually, according to this theory, the two societies will become scarcely distinguishable. It is a rose-colored version of *1984* (which pessimistically saw the two societies developing their bad aspects toward an identical outcome). The basis of the hypothesis of "convergence" is that competition serves as a pressure on the ruling layers of each of the two societies to adopt the best features of the other. In this singularly abstract view of the world of today, such items as the nuclear armaments race are, of course, conveniently left out of consideration, as is the little matter of qualitative leaps in the alleged process of "convergence."

But if we are to advance the hypothesis of a "cold process" for achieving a workers state in countries like Egypt, it would seem quite important to show its difference from the hypothesis of "convergence," the defects of which are rather glaring.

To do this, it is necessary to find a qualitative difference between the two concepts. This can hardly be done by claiming that "convergence" does not operate in the case of the Soviet Union and the United States but does operate in the case of certain countries in the colonial world, although only in one direction—the gradual accumulation of collectivist structures.

The decisive proof that "convergence" will never lead to identity between the USSR and the USA is that the imperialist power would have to undergo a qualitative change, marked by a proletarian revolution. The USSR, on the other hand, would have to undergo a qualitative change in the opposite direction—a social counterrevolution. The alternatives stand in polar contradiction to each other; and some kind of mishmash is excluded.

But the same reasoning holds for any variation applied merely to countries like Egypt. The gradual accumulation of changes in the direction of a workers state would at some point have to pass through a qualitative leap. What is it? Unfortunately, as we have already noted, this is left out of Comrade Maitan's hypothesis. It suffers from the same weakness as the hypothesis of "convergence."

A 'potentially bivalent layer'

The key concept in the hypothesis that perhaps in Egypt and similar countries a workers state might be born through a "cold process" is the idea that the midwife will be the existing state bureaucracy "through the play of factors that have operated up to now."

The state bureaucracy is viewed as a "potentially bivalent layer." It can evolve in either of two directions—either toward a "neocolonialist bureaucracy" or toward "a bureaucracy similar to the bureaucracy of the workers' states." Comrade Maitan calls this hypothesis "the possibility of two variants." The favorable variant would signify that "the class nature of this leadership changes and it can be transformed either into a proletarian-revolutionary leadership or into a bureaucratic worker-peasant leadership."

The majority of the United Secretariat, as Comrade Maitan reports, excluded "the possibility of two variants," limiting themselves "to underlining the conservative character of this layer." In defense of his hypothesis of "two variants," Comrade Maitan offers the analogy of the revolutionary movement in Cuba and certain earlier movements such as the one led by Zapata in Mexico.

What these revolutionary movements have in common with Nasserism is difficult to see. Zapata scarcely represented a conservative state bureaucracy. Castro's course speaks entirely against Comrade Maitan's speculation. Castro organized and led to success a *deep-going popular revolution* and this was one of the essential criteria by which the world Trotskyist movement determined that a workers state had been born in Cuba. Still more—in the process of carrying out this revolution, the petty bourgeois currents that might be considered to be "Nasserist" in character, split away, turned against the revolution, went into exile, and some of them became highly active counter-revolutionaries.[3]

How then did Comrade Maitan happen to bring forward the analogy of movements led by revolutionists like Castro and Zapata? Simply, it would appear, because they began with a radical petty bourgeois ideology. They were of petty bourgeois origin. The Nasser group likewise can be described as of petty bourgeois origin. Clearly the petty bourgeoisie, taken as a whole, is "potentially bivalent." We thus reach the broad generalization that "in the contemporary context . . . it is possible that a petty bourgeois leadership would be submitted to greater 'progressive' pressures and that its 'independent,' 'autonomous' politics would acquire a concrete content quite different from that of the past." In brief, that a class known to be bivalent, can, under the effect of the mounting pressures of today, be more easily pushed in a progressive direction than in the past. Concretely, for example, a Nasserite government may give birth to a deformed workers state through a "cold process."

The main logical defect in this reasoning, as I see it, is the assumption that what is true of a whole is likewise true of its parts. In short, Comrade Maitan does not distinguish between two quite different petty bourgeois tendencies. One is the current that tends to move in the direction of revolutionary socialism. Castro is the outstanding current example of this, but it is not something novel, as Comrade Maitan correctly observes. In fact Marx and Engels themselves were representatives of it. The other current, however, strongly tends to link its fate with capitalism. This variant is not considered by Comrade Maitan; he draws a sharp line between the petty bourgeoisie as a whole and the bourgeoisie as a whole, in face of the fact that the petty bourgeoisie has served historically as a source of origin for the bourgeoisie and is still performing this function in a not inconsiderable way although with much dimmer prospects for many would-be candidates than during the rise of capitalism.

Moreover, Comrade Maitan leaves out of account the fact that if revolutionary pressures have increased enormously on a world scale in recent years, the counter-pressures have likewise mounted. Never before has American imperialism proved itself so ready to intervene in the internal life of other countries by all possible means; never before has the Kremlin proved so passive. These factors powerfully influence the state bureaucracies of the countries in question, even if they seek to find greater elbow room for themselves by playing on international rivalries.

In seeking analogies of real meaning in our effort to understand developments in Egypt and certain other countries, the Mexico of Cárdenas and the Argentina of Perón might offer some fruitful insights. In fact, an illuminating analogy might be found much closer to home—the regime of Muhammad Ali. An account of the efforts of this interesting figure to modernize Egypt may help advance our discussion. We quote from *Egypt in Revolution* by Charles Issawi.

---

3. Comrade Maitan brings forward in connection with his reference to Cuba the absence of a revolutionary socialist party there. But in the theses on Africa the United Secretariat listed the absence of a revolutionary socialist party in Egypt as part of the evidence that under Nasser the masses have not been deeply engaged or mobilized. In the case of Cuba, the masses were mobilized by the Castro team which then moved toward the organization of a revolutionary-socialist party *in the very process of the revolution*. The analogy with Cuba thus speaks once again in opposition to Comrade Maitan's hypothesis. He, most certainly, will not contend that Nasser has given indications of following the example of Castro in either leading a popular revolution, mobilizing the masses and keeping them mobilized, or taking the path to revolutionary Marxism and deciding to organize a revolutionary socialist party.

Muhammad Ali's Egypt

"The 'Founder of Modern Egypt', Muhammad Ali (1805–49), attempted to effect a transition from the subsistence economy prevailing at the beginning of the nineteenth century to a 'modern' complex economy. In this he failed, but instead started Egypt on the road leading to an export-oriented economy. The methods pursued by him are very reminiscent of those used in the Soviet Union and elsewhere in the last forty years.

> First, there was a revolution in the system of land tenure. Tax-farming was abolished and peasants paid their taxes directly to the government; large estates, often of uncultivated land, were granted to relatives or followers of Muhammad Ali; and the prevailing method of communal ownership was replaced by one in which peasants enjoyed *de facto,* though not yet legally recognized, rights of ownership.
>
> Secondly, irrigation works were undertaken, which increased the land under cultivation and, what was more important, made it possible to replace basin irrigation by perennial irrigation and thus produce valuable crops that require summer water.
>
> Thirdly, the planting of long-staple cotton was started on a commercial scale in 1821, and it found ready markets in Europe. By 1824, over 200,000 cantars of cotton were being exported, and in 1845 the figure of 345,000 was reached.
>
> Fourthly, communications were developed, mainly in order to facilitate foreign trade; especially notable were the improvement of the port of Alexandria and its linking by canal to the Nile.
>
> Fifthly, trade was conducted under a system of monopoly. Muhammad Ali bought crops from farmers at low fixed prices and resold them to foreign exporters at great profits. He also directly imported about two-fifths of the goods brought into Egypt.
>
> A similar monopoly was used in an attempt to build up a modern industry. Machinery was imported from Europe together with technicians, and by 1830 factories were turning out cotton, woolen, silk, and linen textiles, sugar, paper, glass, leather, sulphuric acid, and other chemicals. A well-run foundry met the needs of the government armament plants and arsenal, and simple machinery and spare parts were produced. Investments in industrial establishments up to 1838 amounted to about £12 million. Some 30,000–40,000 persons worked in the factories, an impressive figure in a total population of about 3 million, and the number engaged in handicrafts was considerably greater.
>
> The productive apparatus thus built up, with its very large bureaucracy, as well as the army and navy, required men trained in modern techniques. To meet this need, over 300 students were sent to Europe, and several times as many studied in the newly opened schools of medicine, engineering, chemistry, accountancy, and languages and in the military and naval colleges.
>
> In brief, Muhammad Ali was trying to carry out a programme of forced industrialization. His success was thanks primarily to the administrative protection that he gave to his infant industries, which did not, however, outlive that protection. The investment capital required was obtained from the profits of his monopoly of internal and export trade and from taxation and forced loans, and the losses of industrial enterprises were covered from the same sources. The necessary unskilled labour was conscripted and paid low wages, while foreign technicians and skilled workers were attracted by high salaries. A market for the output of the factories was provided by the armed forces, by import substitution, and by displacing some handicrafts.
>
> Other points of resemblance with recent programmes of rapid development should be mentioned. First, the level of living of the population certainly did not rise, and more probably declined, as a result of Muhammad Ali's intensive and often mismanaged investment and of the consequent inflation; the hardships entailed by this and by militarization caused thousands to flee the country in spite of his efforts to seal the frontiers. Nevertheless, a very good case can be made for Muhammad Ali; perhaps unwittingly, but judging from some

of his remarks quite possibly consciously, he was trying to lay the foundation for a balanced, diversified economy that in time would have greatly raised the level of living. However, his prime interest was in building up a modern army and navy to safeguard his position and extend his influence. Hence the compulsory reduction of his armed forces in 1841, following his defeat at the hands of the Great Powers, removed most of the incentive that had made him seek to industrialize Egypt. At the same time the enforcement of the Anglo-Turkish Convention of 1838 permitted foreign traders to buy and sell anywhere within the Ottoman dominions, including Egypt. Simultaneously deprived of Muhammad Ali's protection and encouragement and exposed to the competition of European industry, his factories began to decline and did not survive his death in 1849. (pp. 21–24)

Despite its length, this account, it must be granted, scarcely sounds dated. It should be proof enough that cogent analogies can be found to help illuminate the mysteries of Nasser's Egypt. Muhammad Ali's experiment offers no difficulties to Marxist analysis. It was a case of using the state power to establish conditions for the growth of indigenous capitalism at an otherwise impossible rate. It would not have altered the substance of the matter to put a "socialist" label on the regime.

The reality today

Illuminating as such an analogy may be, it cannot substitute for an analysis of actual developments in Egypt. On this, some pertinent facts can be found in Hassan Riad's book. Despite certain limitations, this is a very good study by an author striving to break out of the sterile pattern of thought imposed by the Egyptian Communist Party.

Of primary importance is the nationalist thrust of the takeovers. They were not undertaken as an essential step in the conscious concretizing of a revolutionary-socialist program. The first holdings to be seized belonged to British, French and Jewish interests (following the imperialist attack by Great Britain, France, and Israel in 1956). The holdings of Belgians, Greeks, Lebanese, Syrians, etc., went next. The ultimate main beneficiary was the Egyptian officer caste represented by Nasser.

The initiative in the 1952 coup d'état which started this process and which Riad calls a "kind of national bourgeois revolution"—with the emphasis on "national," as opposed to foreign interests—came from the "petty bourgeoisie."

"The secret Free Officers Movement of some 250 members was composed of petty bourgeois disappointed in the monarchy or the Wafd and embittered by the defeat in Palestine," he writes. "Although the association included several representatives of the left intellectuals, it was dominated by traditionalists who had rejected Communism out of attachment to their religion. On gaining power, these officers, of modest origin, had no definite program.

"For some years," Riad continues,

> they did what the bourgeoisie would have done if they had had the courage to dethrone Farouk. After all, the West respected the religious traditionalism of the Free Officers and that was enough. The brutal demands of certain Western chancelleries, marked by initiation of the Baghdad pact, the repeated overtures of the Soviet Union, led to the crisis of 1956–57. The problems were settled by force and Egypt won. What followed this test of strength was a real revolution.
>
> Through a bureaucratic process that began in 1953, a new bourgeoisie, of petty bourgeois origin had already been forming. The officers, their relatives and friends grabbed posts in the administration after driving out the aristocrats of the former regime. But things would not have gone very far without the nationalizations of 1957 and the brutal expulsion of the foreigners, which placed the state at the head of the majority of the big enterprises. The managers of the public enterprises took on the role of the big bourgeoisie. It was through this bureaucratic road that the second bourgeois generation was constituted.
>
> In 1957–58, as we have seen, a process of fusion began between this new Nasserite bourgeoisie, of petty bourgeois origin, and the former bourgeoisie of aristocratic origin. (pp. 220–21)

Within the fusion, however, the new elements gained the upper hand, a development that was strengthened by the nationalization of Egyptian enterprises, particularly the key Misr group in 1961. With the "outright expropriation of the former Egyptian big bourgeoisie," the latter now hopes only for the "right to be able to integrate itself in the new state bureaucracy."

As for the current situation in Egypt, Riad paints a sobering picture:

> We have shown that the Egyptian village has not become a place of small proprietors. Despite the agrarian reform, great inequalities remain: 80% of the peasants remain without land or almost without any and only about one-third of their labor power is employed. The political power of the aristocracy, which was formerly based on the intermediate layers, has merely been replaced by that of the state bureaucracy which still bases itself on this relatively privileged minority. The cooperatives, which bring together only the exploiters, that is, 20% of the rural population, constitute in the view of the central power, the transmission belt for the dictatorship of the bureaucracy and the wealthy over the poor rural masses. In the cities, more than half of the population—quasi-permanent unemployed, small craftsmen, subproletariat—are likewise condemned to absolute misery and only one-third of their labor power is employed.
>
> The political power, yesterday in the hands of the bourgeois aristocracy, of Levantine and foreign capital, has passed into the hands of a state bureaucracy. This power is not that of the petty bourgeoisie as a whole, but only a group which has emerged from the petty bourgeoisie, the group of Free Officers and the high civil functionaries linked to them. The form of this new power is state capitalism, which has progressively replaced the liberal capitalism of the bourgeois aristocracy. (pp. 223–24)

As for the rate of growth under Nasser, despite the goals set by the Plan, it has not gone beyond 3% a year. "The best that can be expected is that with the help of quite considerable foreign aid, the Nasserite regime may reach an annual rate of growth of 3.5% to 4%." (p. 225) Three-fourths of this is required to keep up with the expansion of population; the balance goes to the state bureaucracy.

A phenomenon well worth noting is the role of corruption in the state apparatus:

> The corruption . . . is neither a vestige of the past, nor the fruit of deviations nor a sign of objective difficulties in a transition period. It is essential for the functioning of the system itself, an objective law. Of course, corruption was not unknown to either traditional Egypt or the colonialist monarchy. But it was not a central phenomenon of the economic mechanism; the economy was ruled by other objective laws, those of the capitalist market, of profit-seeking, of competition. But the main motor of the economic machine of the Nasserite state is the personal appetite of the rulers and their capacity to create a supporting group. In a system of this kind, corruption, complementing the insufficient remuneration of a bourgeoisie of money-hungry functionaries, becomes an objective necessity. (p. 227)

The state administration is proliferating at a rapid rate. This corresponds to the need to maintain a political equilibrium among the groups formed around the officers who headed the coup d'état.

> It likewise corresponds to the individualist ideology of the petty bourgeois faction that seized power. In a parallel way, a new private bourgeoisie has appeared—businessmen took advantage of the emigration of the Jews to seize important enterprises that had not been nationalized. To do this they had to pay a 'tithe' to the officers by bringing them into their business. In this way a great many dignitaries, under title of managers of state firms, are also interested in private businesses. (p. 88)

The outlines of the tendency to throw up a new bourgeoisie are clearly visible here. This tendency is traced by Riad to the very origin of the regime:

As a matter of fact, the Nasserite bureaucracy did not emerge from a mass movement, from a revolutionary party built in the struggle, but from a coup d'état carried out by a handful of conspirators. They were recruited from above in the existing bodies—the army and the civic administration. To assure their positions, the main dignitaries of the regime built up groups in the same way. Each 'office' was granted by the president to one of his men as a kind of fief to enable him to 'live' and to 'provide a living' for his group. The very language of the members of the regime betrays this concept of the government: *aki ech,* a livelihood. This is the way the nominations accompanying successive reshufflings are characterized. The system remains profoundly individualist: no party discipline limits the abuses and coordinates action. Each one is the sole boss in his domain. Under these conditions, the planning comes to nothing. The Plan is only the day by day addition of desiderata from all sides, without any coherence, without any strategy of development having been worked out beforehand by the higher political bodies. The technicians are then brought in to present as well as possible, in a form meeting propaganda requirements, the whole package of decisions of the leaders of the economic groups on which the political equilibrium of the system rests.

The aspiration for a single party corresponds to the need to create a body to arbitrate the various interests of the ruling groups and their followings. This need, which is felt most keenly by the supreme authority, the president, is ceaselessly counteracted by the bureaucracy. And, in this sense, the failure of the single party reflects the failure of the regime. (pp. 227–228)

Nasser's police regime has aroused the hostility of the proletariat despite some improvements in their position. As for the petty bourgeois masses who were at first favorable, while they have "unquestionably been affected by the religious, chauvinist, pan-Arabic and reactionary propaganda, they have remained, as a whole, hostile to the regime, or at least apathetic." (p. 231)

Riad's hypothesis

In the light of this reality, how should we characterize Nasser's Egypt? Hassan Riad had definite opinions on the subject. He believes we are dealing with a case of "state capitalism" and the rise of a "new local ruling class." (p. 238). His concept of this class is not clearly presented and it is hard to tell whether he believes it is a mere transitional phase in the gestation of a new bourgeoisie of the standard type or whether it is something utterly new and unforeseen, like the "managerial class" which was once in vogue among radical intellectuals as a label for the Soviet bureaucracy. Riad, however, states flatly that Egypt "is not on the road to becoming a people's democracy . . ." (p. 228) which would imply that he visualizes "state capitalism" in Egypt as a forcing bed for a bourgeoisie comparable to the one in Mexico or Argentina.

He does see the state bureaucracy in Egypt as a "third type" of bureaucracy, different from both the state bureaucracy analyzed many times over by the Marxists and from the bureaucracies of the workers states of Europe and Asia. Moreover, he sees this "third type" of bureaucracy as a rather widespread phenomenon:

> In a certain number of African and Asian countries, of which Nasserite Egypt without doubt constitutes the most important example, the political power has been monopolized by a new bureaucracy emerging after independence is won. Circumstances have permitted petty bourgeois groups to seize power for themselves. These groups then became transformed into a bureaucracy which, when they succeed in statizing the economy as in Egypt, become genuine possessing classes, of a new type, incapable, due to their origin, of preparing the passage over to genuine socialism. (p. 226)

In the long run, in Riad's opinion, the "state bourgeoisie" can only become an "appendage in the Third World to the imperialist bourgeois, replacing the former local ruling classes which it dethroned in a more or less radical way, in their role as intermediary, local agent of imperialism." (p. 240)

The incapacity of this "new-type" bureaucracy to open the way to socialism is ascribable in Riad's opinion to the "reactionary ideology" inherited by the new bureaucracy from its history and origin.

Of the various flaws in Riad's study, we have room to mention only one which is especially pertinent to the question under examination. The category of a degenerated or deformed workers state is missing from the conceptual framework of his analysis. This leads to some curious results.

Riad has no trouble, of course, in determining a normal workers state on the basis of economic, sociological and political characteristics as a whole. But what about an abnormal one?

He hinges everything on the nature of the bureaucracy. If it is a good bureaucracy on the whole, it is a workers state. If it is a bad bureaucracy on the whole, it is not.

Thus, in the case of the Soviet Union, which he defends as "socialist," he is compelled to idealize the bureaucracy. It is "linked to the masses," he declares, and is "animated" by a highly modern and progressive "ideology," and is building a "fully and genuinely socialist society" (p. 226) "despite the excesses of Stalin" (p. 242). His criteria for a workers state quite clearly include a "revolutionary proletarian ideology" among the ruling layer. Thus he is led to say: "The fate of the bureaucratic privileged Soviet elite has always been linked, by their historic origin, to the construction of socialism. Their attachment, despite all the deformations due to them, to the revolutionary proletarian ideology testifies to this historic origin and this solidarity in fact." (p. 242)

In a quite logical way, Riad makes this subjective criterion the key one for determining the character of the state in Egypt. Despite the veneer of "socialist" phraseology, the ruling caste is in substance capitalist in its outlook, in his opinion. Despite the apparently "socialist" form given to the economy by the nationalizations, this caste has fused with the old bourgeoisie and is utilizing the state in the general interests of a new capitalist ruling class in formation, one which will eventually clearly prove itself to be an appendage of Western imperialism.

On purely formal grounds it could be argued that Riad would have difficulty countering the position that Egypt "as of now" should be considered to be a deformed workers state on the basis of the extensive nationalizations. However, Riad would clearly carry the day on the basis of his concrete data on the sociological composition of the ruling layers and the direction of their evolution.

The trend is clear

The final answer to Riad's views on the nature of Nasser's Egypt will, of course, be provided by reality itself, and here we may resume our discussion with Comrade Maitan. If Marxist theory is worth anything at all as a weapon in the class struggle, it is in providing timely prevision of the future. Comrade Maitan's point is that in forecasting the future, we must leave open the variant of a "bivalent" bureaucracy in Egypt (and elsewhere) which can turn in either of two directions—toward sowing a new bourgeoisie or toward giving birth to a workers state. He agrees that the latter variant has not as yet appeared anywhere; moreover that the state bureaucracy is conservative. We have cited considerable evidence from an authority on Egypt, who has made a close and conscientious study, showing that the trend is not toward the establishment of a workers state in Egypt under Nasser's rule. *The evidence is just the contrary.* If we project the current trend of the bureaucratic layer, subjected to the pressure of the status quo and its own interests, it is quite clear that what will emerge in Egypt eventually is a new bourgeoisie, one that was fostered and promoted by the capitalist state now existing in Egypt. Why shouldn't the Fourth International forecast this variant and exclude from an official resolution a hypothesis that is supported by neither past experience, current evidence nor solid theoretical considerations?

Taking another look at Comrade Maitan's hypothesis in the light of the above considerations, it would seem that it is not unrelated to Riad's thesis about the appearance of a new type bureaucracy, which can emerge from the petty bourgeoisie. Riad puts a negative sign on this bureaucracy, rejecting the possibility that it can open the way to what he calls a "people's democracy." Comrade Maitan, starting from virtually the same premise, foresees instead a possible variant on which a positive sign must be placed—precisely because it is petty bourgeois, it can prove responsive to class pressures of opposing kinds and thus go in either the neocolonialist direction, to which Riad limits it, or in a proletarian direction.

The chief flaw in this hypothesis, as I have sought to show, is that it leaves out specific origins, thus lumping together groups emerging from the officer caste of the bourgeois state and plebeian revolutionaries who begin, for example, with guerrilla warfare. The two are far from identical. Associated with this is the assumption, it appears to me, that purely objective factors can override even political consciousness so that a workers state could be born despite the contrary intentions of its founders and without the intervention of the masses. There is a tendency here, I feel, to separate out the objective factors, to give them a certain independence and therefore a weight they do not possess. The objective factors must still operate through class forces which respond according to their own intrinsic dynamics. That is why the historic tasks of the working class cannot be performed by the petty bourgeoisie although the working class can carry out tasks properly belonging to older classes that have retrogressed. The undue delay of the proletarian revolution in the imperialist centers has, of course, given rise to all kinds of distortions and anomalies on a world scale, but the interrelationship between the objective and subjective factors still holds true in all its main lines including the birth of workers states.

I leave aside other flaws, belonging more properly to the political level, involving the perspectives of the movement and how Comrade Maitan's hypothesis affects these. Although they are extremely important, they are derivative if we approach the subject from its theoretical side.

There is one implication in Comrade Maitan's hypothesis, however, that can hardly be overlooked. If it is possible for the state bureaucracy in countries like Egypt to set up a deformed workers state in a "cold way," what is really wrong with the hypothesis that the state bureaucracy in a country like the Soviet Union can set up proletarian democracy in a "cold way"? One of the main assumptions in both hypotheses appears to be pretty much the same; i.e., that the state bureaucracy can prove responsive enough to objective pressures to undertake progressive modifications that willy-nilly cross the point of qualitative change.

I do not at all wish to give the impression that Comrade Maitan has changed his mind about the way proletarian democracy will be restored in the Soviet Union—through a political revolution undertaken by the masses. I simply call attention to an important logical implication of his hypothesis concerning inherently progressive possibilities in state bureaucracies in a considerable belt of countries.

'Statism' and the officer caste

(1) The history of Egypt goes back in unbroken continuity for six or seven thousand years. During this immense time, as in other "hydraulic societies," the state always played a dominant role in the economy. "The tendency toward unity, centralism, concentration, a pyramidal hierarchy, reached into all domains," writes Anouar Abdel-Malek in *Egypte Société Militaire*. "The power, master of the water, also held the land, which it consented, at times, to place in usufruct with those whom it favored. The central state tolerated no provincialism, no feudal system; the Mamelukes themselves, once they conquered power in Cairo, hastened . . . to undertake responsibility . . . for what the Egyptian state could not neglect without ruining the source of everything—the life-giving water. . . . The state, master of the political power, whose head was the incarnation or the representative of the divinity, held in its hands the economic system, of which it was the sole possessor throughout history until capitalism erupted, three-quarters of a century ago." (p. 338)

How should something going back to the Pharaohs be weighed in estimating current trends in Egypt? Has capitalism, imposed relatively recently by foreign imperialist interests, completely destroyed the age-old tradition in such a short time? This seems dubious. The life of the peasants still centers on the land and its relation to the Nile. Throughout the capitalist period the maintenance and extension of the irrigation system has been given high priority by the state. The Nasser regime has, if anything, placed even greater stress on public works as the High Dam eloquently testifies. The insistence of most commentators on the role of Egypt's "population explosion" in Nasser's projects tends to obscure this background.

If Egypt's ancient pattern remains as at least a psychological heritage, can it be said to favor the creation of a workers state without a basic upheaval emanating from the exploited masses? No doubt the Egyptian people are predisposed to accept strong public regulation of their economic life, even to view it as a natural necessity; yet the deep conservatism of this tradition would seem to favor development of a new exploiting class in continuation of the old—a national bourgeoisie imbued from birth to see the state as the chief instrument for safeguarding and advancing its own general interests, which are also bound up with extensive public works. The possibility of a Muhammad Ali would appear to have deeper sources than just pure accident.

(2) In Egypt, as in a number of other countries, we are confronted with extreme instances of "statism" (the term Trotsky preferred in contradistinction to "state capitalism," which long ago lost really precise meaning). This is an important development that deserves careful study on the theoretical level as well as active political attention. In the final analysis, the monstrous growth of statism is a symptom of the overripeness of capitalism for socialism. An increasing number of countries have no alternative but to mobilize the state power for economic ends even if these are still held within the confining and chaotic orbit of capitalism. The main lesson to be drawn from Nasser's Egypt is the ease with which a deep-going popular revolution there could put a workers and peasants government in power, with reverberations far exceeding those of the Cuban revolution.

(3) The role of the officer caste, or a sector of it, in advancing "statism" in the colonial and semicolonial countries is significant. It has been a prominent feature all the way from the Mexico of Cárdenas and the Argentina of Perón to Nasser's Egypt and Ne Win's Burma. While the bulk of the military figures involved are of petty bourgeois origin (upper petty bourgeois generally) the army, as an institution, acts in these circumstances as the rather naked embodiment of the bourgeois state.

The officer caste intervenes in trying to solve the overall economic and political problems of the bourgeoisie, bringing to the task a certain ruthlessness, characteristic of the military mind, and a readiness to resort to desperate measures and dangerous gambles. They may even provide openings which revolutionary-socialist forces could turn to advantage. Cárdenas expropriated the oil industry and turned it over to management by the trade unions, following it up with similar measures for the railways. Perón quite consciously headed the formation of mass trade unions. It would be a considerable mistake, however, to conclude from this that the officer caste of a bourgeois army can inaugurate a workers state. The virulent "anti-Communism," only too prevalent among these careerist-minded layers is not without its reason.

(4) The greatly increased role of the officer caste, as witnessed in many countries today, may have progressive consequences at times, but these remain uncertain at best. The military institution tends to become more and more inordinate in size and pretensions, absorbing an ever greater share of the national budget. That this serves legitimate national defense needs is largely pretense; what is most significant is the tendency to foster reactionary currents in the internal life of the nation. An often repeated pattern has been the strengthening of the ultra-right-wing formations in the army itself. At a certain point these can erupt with startling speed, and completely reverse—at least for a time—what appeared to be a gradual evolution in a promising direction. It would be fatal to overlook this very real possibility in certain countries. Recent events in Algeria should serve as a serious warning on this.

(5) It is not excluded that history will eventually offer an example of a workers state being born in a relatively painless way. After the United States, Great Britain, Japan, France, Germany, and Italy have gone socialist, it may well be likely that the rulers of a country like Iceland (if they have not already been retired to a balmier climate) will decide to bid for the honor of being the first ruling class to willingly retire from the scene. Speculation on such pleasant possibilities, however, should not be permitted to affect the task of establishing the necessary preliminary conditions. This involves some quite recalcitrant formations.

3. The Algerian revolution and the character of the Ben Bella regime

After the fall of the radical regime of Ahmed Ben Bella in July 1965, the Fourth International undertook to evaluate the phases of the Algerian revolution and the role played by Trotskyists in it. The following letter written in 1969 by Joseph Hansen was part of a discussion on this. The resolution on "The Algerian Revolution from 1962 to 1969," that was adopted subsequent to this discussion, appears in the second section of this collection. The letter is published for the first time.

January 9, 1969

Dear Comrades,

On the proposed Algerian resolution.

First of all, the draft includes what appears to me to be acceptable and informative material concerning (a) the developments since the Boumedienne coup in 1965, and (b) the current situation.

Also, the suggested planks for an immediate program appear to me to be correct in general.

If these sections were separated out and the others were edited accordingly, the resolution would encounter little opposition, I am sure.

Two threads of argumentation in the document are certain to be disputed, however. The first concerns what the text describes as "points of disagreement" at the 1965 world congress which today "seem secondary and of purely historical importance"; i.e., the characterization of the Ben Bella government and the estimate of the import of the Boumedienne coup. (End of Section I and beginning of Section II.) If these questions were genuinely secondary and of purely historical importance, they could profitably be considered in a separate resolution or raised in a signed article. However, later in the document the problem of the characterization of the Ben Bella government is viewed somewhat differently; i.e., "there is nothing academic in our taking up this question." (Section VI, paragraph 1.)

The second item that is certain to be disputed is the self-criticism of the course followed by the leadership of the Fourth International. The idea of undertaking a self-criticism is good, but it demands thoroughness and a correct axis, both of which are missing, in my opinion.

Taking up these points in order—

If I understand the underlying thesis of the document correctly, the Fourth International was led into an overly optimistic appraisal of the possibilities inherent in the Algerian revolution because of two errors in theory.

One of these errors was to suppose that the hypothesis advanced at the Fourth Congress of the Communist International in 1922 was applicable to the Algeria of 1962–65; that is, that in a situation like the one in 1962 in Algeria a workers and peasants government—a petty-bourgeois government resting on a capitalist state structure which nevertheless points in the direction of a workers state,—can come into existence without having been initiated by a revolutionary Marxist party.

The other error in theory was to draw an analogy between the revolutionary process in Algeria and the revolutionary process in Cuba where a workers state was established.

Because of these two errors in theory, the underlying thesis of the resolution holds, not only did the leadership of the Fourth International come to place exaggerated hopes in the revolutionary situation in Algeria, it was led into committing some further errors: (a) exaggerating the achievements registered under Ben Bella, and (b) minimizing the seriousness of certain unfavorable events.

By way of self-criticism, it is necessary, in accordance with this thesis, to correct the theoretical errors that were committed. This means, specifically, recognizing that the designation of the Ben Bella government as a "workers and peasants government" was wrong. In place of that designation, a correct label should be placed on it; namely . . . Namely? Here, unfortunately, the resolution becomes vague. All I can find in the document by way of answer is the label, "Jacobin team."

In what way does this label improve things on the theoretical level? The benefits ought to be at least noticeable since the label is a costly one: (1) It cuts the continuity in theory which we have drawn with the hypothesis made by the Bolsheviks and leaves us with the problem of finding a theory other than the one advanced at the Fourth Congress to account for the kind of government that appeared in Algeria. (2) It destroys our theory of what happened in Cuba, denies the parallel nature of the processes in the two countries, and prevents us from understanding on the theoretical level how the two revolutions could have a reciprocal influence.

But the benefits escape me. Did this "Jacobin team" function as a government? The answer, of course, is that it did. What was the class nature of this "Jacobin team" government? The answer is "petty bourgeois." Did it rest on a capitalist state structure? The answer is "yes." Did it nevertheless undertake measures which if pursued to their logical conclusion would have ended in the establishment of a workers state in Algeria? The answer is "yes."

Four questions, along with their necessary answers, are sufficient to establish that so far as *content* is concerned, the label "Jacobin team," as applied to the Ben Bella regime, designates precisely the same phenomena as the label "workers and peasants government." Moreover, this is without insisting on what was widely agreed at the time—how this government was influenced by the Cuban example, and what striking parallels existed between the Cuban and Algerian revolutions.

The sole justification advanced by the author of the resolution in arguing for this new label is the following consideration: "It must in fact be noted that all the variants of a workers and peasants government cited in the theses of the Fourth Congress of the Communist International in 1922 assumed that all these governments would be composed of representatives of mass workers *parties*."

This misses the key point made by the Fourth Congress; namely, that these parties would be *petty bourgeois*. As we well know, petty-bourgeois formations, whether they call themselves a "party" or a "movement" (like the National Liberation Front or the July 26 Movement) are kaleidoscopic. The word "party" in this context, does not correspond to anything in reality substantially distinct from what the petty bourgeoisie is capable of organizing in the political arena under a different name.

The proof of this, so far as the Fourth Congress is concerned, is that the Bolsheviks excluded the possibility of such formations actually establishing a workers state. They gave no special credit to their capacities because of the "party" label attached to them.

What is new in the objective reality is that one such formation, the July 26 Movement, did actually establish a workers state.

Observe now what theoretical problems and difficulties are raised by the resolution in attempting to "rectify" the supposed errors made with regard to Algeria. "But it should be noted," declares the author of the resolution in arguing that the 1922 hypothesis of the Bolsheviks was not applicable to Algeria, "that the concept of a workers and peasants government was formulated by the Communist International at the start of the general capitalist crisis and prior to the development of the colonial revolution (before even the Chinese revolution). Therefore, it could not foresee that because of the weakening of world capitalism, colonial regimes could be overthrown by Jacobin teams not yet possessing revolutionary parties." (Section VI, paragraph 9.) If we apply this to Cuba, as we must since its revolution was part of the colonial revolution, it follows that a "Jacobin team not yet possessing a revolutionary party" can establish a *workers state!* But the author in the very same paragraph boggles at admitting the possibility that a "Jacobin team not yet possessing a revolutionary party" can establish something much less—a workers and peasants government. Thus the resolution eliminates from our theory of the Cuban revolution an essential link in our theoretical appreciation of the course it took, our estimate of the nature of the transitional government which actually existed in Cuba before the establishment of the workers state.

In short, the resolution, if passed, would deal a serious blow to the theoretical work achieved by our movement in this area.

To continue. The July 26 Movement, a "Jacobin team not yet possessing a revolutionary party," succeeded in establishing a workers and peasants government which in turn made it possible to establish a workers state in Cuba. In Algeria, the Ben Bella wing of the National Liberation Front, a "Jacobin team not yet possessing a revolutionary party," succeeded in establishing a workers and peasants government which did *not* realize the possibility of establishing a workers state. The process was cut off and a defeat was suffered. If we examine what happened in Algeria in the light of what the Bolsheviks projected in 1922, then it must be admitted that the outcome in Algeria came much closer to the Bolshevik forecast than the outcome in Cuba. A certain credit is due the Bolsheviks for their prescience in this instance. Or, looked at from another angle, weighty evidence, although of a negative nature, is provided for the paragraph in the major resolution for the coming world congress which notes a shift in today's revolutionary pattern "closer to the classical norm of proletarian revolutions." (Last paragraph of Section I.)

What was the reason for the failure of the workers and peasants government to establish a workers state in Algeria? Exactly as the Bolsheviks said, *the absence of a revolutionary Marxist party*. I will return to this.

In order to maintain his underlying thesis, the author of the draft resolution on Algeria is compelled, despite his own intentions, to play down the three-year period, 1962–65. "These considerations are by no means intended," he says, "to minimize the real advances which marked the development of the Algerian revolution during the first years after independence. They are not intended either to denigrate the real anti-imperialist and anticapitalist actions of the Ben Bella government and, more precisely, the limited team around Ben Bella, which [note in the next phrase how the achievements are minimized] on several occasions went outside the institutional framework to make concessions to the masses." The minimizing is evident again in the next sentence which is intended to be laudatory: "The process of legalizing the conquests of the masses by decrees, going beyond the established institutions, is an example of this."

After reading this draft resolution, I went back to the files of *World Outlook* to see what had been published there. Obviously the reporting of events there, as in the other publications of the Trotskyist movement during that period, does not match the present impressions of the author. But I would contend that the reflection of the events in the pages of our press comes closer to the reality.

Big mobilizations *did* occur under the leadership of Ben Bella. Far-reaching measures *were* enacted. There was very good reason for holding open the possibility that the Algerian revolution might take a course similar to the one followed by the Cuban revolution. We were not the only ones to see things that way. It was widely feared by the bourgeoisie on an international scale. And, in fact, the outcome could only be determined by the actual struggle itself.

The reasons why a socialist victory did not occur are clear enough, I think. (1) The French bourgeoisie had learned a salutary lesson from the American experience with Cuba (and their own experiences in Vietnam and elsewhere); they gave up the attempt to crush the rebellion by main force and shifted instead to a policy of trying to subvert it. (2) Ben Bella was no Fidel Castro, Houari Boumedienne no Che Guevara. (The subjective element was an important factor.) (3) There was no revolutionary Marxist party.

Our reporting of the events, and our theoretical appreciation of the broad outlines of the process of the Algerian revolution stand up very well, in my opinion. It is only necessary to bring our analysis up to date and make some minor corrections.

The resolution notes that in 1965 one of the differences at the world congress was over the nature of the June 19 coup, some of the comrades (mostly those working in Algeria) maintaining that no qualitative change had occurred. (Section I, point 5.) These differences have not been settled, according to the resolution: "Subsequently, the majority agreed that the coup was the qualitative expression of a molecular deterioration which had occurred in the last period of Ben Bella's regime." It should, therefore, be possible to record in a resolution without much debate that the coup of June 19, 1965, marked a qualitative change. Boumedienne smashed the workers and peasants government. He established a different kind of government, one headed in a different general direction from that taken by the Ben Bella regime when it came to power.

It is a correct assessment that when the Ben Bella regime did not carry things forward to establishment of a workers state, a process of deterioration set in. (This is where a correction is to be made in our previous analysis.) Right after the June 19 coup, we called that event the turning point, although we had already noted the stagnation that had set in under Ben Bella and had called attention to the danger it represented. In retrospect, it is clear that the *turn* in direction came earlier than June 19; it came with the period of stagnation. Ben Bella began making concessions to the right at the expense of the Trotskyists and their allies. He turned away from mass mobilizations to extreme reliance on clique maneuvering, narrowed down his base of support, and assumed extraordinary personal powers. Today it should not be difficult to establish the approximate date when the movement began to subside. The deterioration became more and more marked until the Ben Bella regime lost its "socialist option," a fact registered qualitatively by the June 19 coup. The contradiction between the capitalist state and the socialist orientation of the government was removed by Boumedienne. His regime reflects rather faithfully the capitalist state structure on which it rests.

In passing, I note that the resolution in mentioning the 1962 crisis says that this culminated in the victory of the "Ben Bella-Boumedienne team." (Section I, point 2.) But in rereading the material written at the time, the two men were not presented as a combination of equals like this. Throughout the 1962–65 period, Boumedienne remained in the background, an enigmatic figure whose real political coloration failed to stand out. This also accounts for the immense surprise all circles felt over the coup (with the exception of Paris and possibly Washington), as well as the general disbelief (particularly in the left-wing fringes of the Algerian government apparatus) that any decisive change had occurred. Evidently, as the deterioration set in, Boumedienne's weight as a political figure mounted while Ben Bella's declined.

As to the nature of the Boumedienne regime, it resembles a good many others of the newly "independent" countries. Its strong military coloration and direct intervention in the economy masks a nascent bourgeoisie gestating in the government apparatus. What is decisive, as in the case of Egypt, is the direction of its development, its consciousness of this direction, its ties with the old bourgeoisie and the imperialists, the extent to which it is able to maintain and divert the flow of surplus value into private channels, and, above all, its correspondence with the capitalist state structure on which it rests.

In light of this, the following sentence is misleading: "Given the social and political weakness of the Algerian bourgeoisie, this state bureaucracy has proved to be more of a danger to the Algerian revolution than the bourgeoisie itself." (Section IV, paragraph 1.) All kinds of interpretations could be placed on this, none of which, I am sure, are shared or intended by the author of the resolution. I think there will be no problem in adjusting this and similar small things in the resolution once the main points are corrected, particularly since the analysis of the composition of the state bureaucracy appears to me to be rather good.

The most instructive aspect of the entire development in Algeria is that a workers and peasants government could appear, bearing many resemblances to the one in the early stages of the Cuban revolution, but which, unlike the Cuban formation, was unable to carry the revolution forward to the establishment of a workers state. This experience calls for a critical examination of all aspects of the Algerian revolution, including the fact that a successful armed struggle—a successful guerrilla war, if you like—*does not necessarily lead to a socialist victory.*

This conclusion is reinforced by one of the observations in the resolution which is adduced to back up a criticism of the estimates made at the time by the leadership of the Fourth International:

> The masses of poor peasants could have offered a broader social base, but they were atomized during the crisis of the summer of 1962. These masses have not been able to mobilize themselves to this day. The Fourth International did not correctly weigh the importance of this void and therefore tended not to see this major difference between the situation in Algeria and the situation which led to the establishment of a workers state in Cuba less than two years after the Castroist team took power. (Section VI, paragraphs 3 and 4.)

The criticism is invalid, it appears to me, because the importance of this void *was* weighed at the time and it led the Fourth International to place heavy emphasis on the need to mobilize the masses as was done by the Castroist team in Cuba. But leaving that aside, what is really said in these sentences? *That the mobilization of the peasantry in an armed struggle was not sufficient to achieve a socialist victory in Algeria.* After the country's "independence" was won, the peasantry became atomized and they have not been able to mobilize themselves since then. For a socialist victory in Algeria, something more was needed than an armed struggle plus the mobilization of the peasantry.

This lesson is of considerable importance, it appears to me, and well worth thinking about. Obviously it does not change the conclusion that a socialist victory is inconceivable in situations like the one in Algeria without an armed struggle and the mobilization of the peasantry. But something more than that is required; namely, a revolutionary Marxist party, a Leninist combat party. This, then, must never be lost sight of in projecting strategy and tactics from here on out.

It also provides the proper axis, I would think, for engaging in self-criticism with regard to the participation of the Fourth International in the Algerian revolution. The involvement of the Trotskyist movement in the underground struggle, in aiding the guerrillas, in backing the workers and peasants government that came to power in 1962 was exemplary. Individual members served heroically. The movement as a whole took correct general positions.

But what was accomplished in carrying out its specific function as the bearer of the tradition and know-how of building a Leninist combat party? This is what has to be answered in any serious self-criticism once we have shown that the missing link in the Algerian revolution was a combat party.

What was done, for instance, to recruit Algerian militants to the Trotskyist movement? What was done on a day-to-day basis? Deliberately done to single out possible cadres, win them over organizationally, indoctrinate them, and train them in the art of organizing a combat party? How did the Trotskyist fractions operate? How well did they compete with other political tendencies in garnering members? What were the particular problems in the complicated Algerian struggle bearing on this question? What was done to meet them? What kind of transitional formations were tried to help solve these problems? What lessons were learned that could be passed on? How well was the living chain of cadres actually forged?

I simply indicate the kind of questions that should be raised and answered in a serious self-criticism. The subject is quite concrete and requires concrete information to be dealt with adequately. It devolves on those who were engaged in this work to draw the lessons.

I would venture only a general impression—one in which I may be mistaken, since I was not directly involved in this work and do not know the details. My impression is that the tactics called for in the first period—of becoming integrated in the mass movement at any cost—were carried forward without much change in succeeding periods, after our comrades had become well integrated and had, in fact, established first-rate reputations on a rather broad scale. They continued to serve as helpers and handmaidens for the mass movement. They did not make a timely turn and put the seemingly narrow interests of the Trotskyist movement, the Trotskyist movement in and of itself, first on the agenda, making demands on the mass movement (or at least responsive sectors of it) to understand the importance of the Fourth International as an organization and the imperativeness of contributing in an adequate material way to building a strong Algerian section. The error was at best an instance of organizational inertia, tactical rigidity, perhaps a misconception of the role of the party, or, at worst, an opportunist adaptation first to the limitations of the guerrilla movement and then the Ben Bella regime.

To repeat. With the benefit of being able now to look back at the course of events and the actual pattern of the revolution, and seeing that what was decisive for victory or defeat was the existence or nonexistence of a revolutionary Marxist party, how well did the Fourth International fulfill its duty in this respect, on the *organizational* level?

To be still more concrete, given the small forces which the movement had to begin with and the imperative necessity of integrating them in the mass struggle, what was done in the succeeding period, when an opportunity opened that was among the most brilliant in the history of our movement, to realize what was actually possible; i.e., the construction—not of a Jacobin team—but of a Trotskyist team, the decisive link in the process of building a revolutionary Marxist party in this situation?

Was any error committed such as thinking that it was sufficient to merely launch an armed struggle, merely mobilize the peasantry, merely organize material aid, merely support a Jacobin team, without bearing constantly in mind, day in and day out, how these activities were being translated into hard organizational gains and the construction of a Trotskyist team?

Any specific actions undertaken by our comrades, which it is now felt ought to be criticized, should be viewed in the light of these considerations. How did the actions that were engaged in this work help or hinder the party-building process? For instance, calling for a "left led by the FLN" (Section V, last paragraph), or minimizing the Khider "attack on the UGTA congress"? (Section VI, paragraph 6.)

Whether these or other specific items were really errors, and, if so, whether they were minor, considerable, or gross errors, can only be determined by viewing them in relation to the actual work of party building in Algeria. And in assessing the nature and seriousness of the errors, responsibility should be determined in a definite way and not placed at the door of the movement as a whole, where responsibility resides chiefly on the political level.

In my opinion, primary responsibility rests with Pablo, who was deeply involved in the situation and who should have known what the key links are in the process of building a combat party. I think that he failed to represent the interests of the Trotskyist movement as they should have been represented in this situation. Whether a different course could have altered the final outcome is, naturally, speculative. But the error in orientation—if such it was—did not help matters.

In this connection, one wonders how a sentence like the following ever got into the resolution:

At the World Reunification Congress in July 1963, although this work was directed by cadres belonging to a tendency that was subsequently to leave the main stream of the movement, it was approved unanimously by the movement's highest authority. (Section VI, paragraph 1.)

The sentence should either be eliminated or changed to state without euphemisms that the work was directed by Pablo, who subsequently split from the movement when it called him to account for gross violations of discipline.

Otherwise, it seems to me that the way the reunification was handled is brought into question. What is implied is that accounts should have been settled with Pablo at the Reunification Congress. Was that possible then? Or even desirable? Should the door have been closed in 1963 to the possibility of Pablo becoming part of the new leadership of the Fourth International and accepting its discipline in Algeria? In my opinion, it would have been dead wrong to do that.

In recasting the resolution, a couple of small things should be caught. In the copy we received, there is no section "III"; there are two sections numbered "VI". A company in Algeria is spelled three different ways: "Sonatrack," "Sonatrach," and "Sonabrach." It would be helpful to list the name of every organization or body which is at present referred to by mysterious letters. In resolutions of this nature we ought to bear in mind that not all our members are old specialists in Algerian affairs. Some, in fact, are rather new recruits who appreciate being helped in learning the argot of the movement.

Comradely,
Joseph Hansen

4. The social transformations in Eastern Europe, China, and Cuba

In a report to the twenty-third national convention of the Socialist Workers Party in August 1969, Joseph Hansen presented a general review of the characteristics of the post–World War Two overturns in property relations, with particular attention to the case of China. The following is an excerpt from that talk.

At the time of the victory of the Chinese Revolution over Chiang Kai-shek and his imperialist backers, our movement was confronted with the necessity to explain the contradiction between certain long-held theoretical postulates and the actual course of events. The postulates were as follows:

1. The peasantry as a class cannot lead a revolutionary struggle through to a successful conclusion.
2. This can be achieved only by the proletariat.
3. The proletariat cannot do it except by organizing a revolutionary Marxist party.
4. Stalinism does not represent revolutionary Marxism; in essence it is counterrevolutionary.
5. Stalinism represents a temporary retrogression in the first workers state; the advance of the revolution will doom it and it will not reappear.

Despite these postulates, which appeared to have been thoroughly established by both weighty theoretical considerations and a mountain of empirical evidence, in the Chinese Revolution the proletariat did not play a leading role as a class. Instead, this role was assumed by the peasantry.

Moreover, no revolutionary Marxist party was formed on a mass scale. Instead, a Stalinist party stood at the head of the revolutionary forces and came to power in a struggle that ultimately toppled capitalism.

Finally, Stalinism was quite consciously cultivated by the new regime. Today this school of thought has culminated in a cult of the personality that if anything has outdone its model in the Soviet Union.

The problem that faced our movement was to explain these contradictions and to determine what lessons should be drawn and what they portended for the future.

So far as the *political* positions of the world Trotskyist movement were concerned, no problem existed. Without exception our positions were correct, ranging from full support to China, despite Chiang Kai-shek, in the struggle against Japanese imperialism to full support for the revolution against Chinese capitalism and the vestiges of feudalism despite the Stalinist nature of the leadership that was thrown to the forefront.

It is very important to remember this, for it constitutes the most positive kind of proof that our movement is a dynamic political formation and not a church dedicated to maintaining the purity of a set of dogmas. One can feel proud in reading the political platforms presented in the documents of that time. They were very good, standing up remarkably well under the test of events.

Problem of the proletarian content

As to the attempts to find solutions to the contradictions between the reality and our theoretical postulates, some of these were clearly in error from the beginning. Others have not held up, or only created fresh difficulties.

In the main, the attempted solutions centered around locating the proletarian content which it was felt must lie at the heart of the Chinese Revolution despite its strange forms and the role of Stalinism.

For instance, in the case of the peasantry, there was speculation that perhaps its true nature had been misjudged. Unlike the peasants of Western Europe and elsewhere, perhaps the Chinese peasants had achieved a proletarian or even socialist consciousness either because of the peculiarities of China's historic background or because of the impact of imperialism on the country.

A current example of this line of thought is to be found in Comrade Moreno's contribution in *Fifty Years of World Revolution*.

Much greater attention was paid to the nature of the Chinese Communist Party. This was only natural since our movement from its very inception has considered the question of the party to be primordial in the process of bringing a revolution to victory. Thus it appeared that the key to the success in China must be sought in the nature of the Chinese Communist Party.

One line of speculation was that Trotsky had made a mistake in concluding that the Chinese Communist Party under Mao had become a peasant party.

Another was that if Trotsky had been right in his conclusion at the time, then it must have changed back into a proletarian organization.

Comrade Morris Stein argued, for instance, if I recall correctly, that there was a steady flow of workers from the cities who went into the countryside and joined the Chinese Communist Party. Their influence, he thought, was sufficient to give a proletarian character to the party.

Another line of speculation concerned the personal qualities and influence of Mao Tse-tung. Some comrades felt that despite everything, when Mao Tse-tung was faced by the supreme test, he had adhered in practice, if not in program, propaganda, or diplomacy, to revolutionary Marxism.

Still another variant was that the very Stalinism of the Chinese Communist Party gave it a proletarian character. The line of thought here was that Stalinism is connected with the workers state in the Soviet Union and that this association therefore makes it proletarian.

At bottom, this view represents an *identification* of Stalinism with the workers state. It is quite a change from Trotsky's position that Stalinism stands in *contradiction* to the workers state, that it is a cancerous growth. As against the *proletarian* tendency represented by Leninism and the Left Opposition, Trotsky considered Stalinism to be *petty-bourgeois* in nature.

Another line of thought, flowing in the same general channel of trying to find something proletarian about the Chinese Communist Party, was the view that this party changed from a peasant party to a "centrist" party, then a "left centrist" party, then an "opportunist workers party," and finally a "workers party."

In the current discussion, the view that Mao's policies should be designated as "bureaucratic centrism" may fall within this frame.

While I am on the point, I should like to say that I fail to see what is gained by this nomenclature. If we ask what is the class nature of "centrism," whatever its variety, we are compelled to say that it is petty-bourgeois. That is also the class nature of Stalinism. It is petty-bourgeois.

Thus the introduction of the general term "centrism" does not help in answering whether a Stalinist party can become a revolutionary party. It merely suggests a succession of stages in which the class essence of the gradation or series of steps remains obscure.

Marcy, Swabeck, Posadas, and Healy

It was quite clear from the beginning that all these tentative answers to the central problem carried implications that could prove quite dangerous politically; and we were soon to experience repercussions in our ranks. I will mention some of them.

Sam Marcy and his group rapidly came to the conclusion that Stalinism in power equals a workers state. Since a Stalinist party had gained power in China, this signified that a workers state had been established.

From this position, Marcy evolved into a Maoist of such fervor that he was capable of swallowing even the new constitution, announced at the Ninth Congress of the Chinese Communist Party, designating Lin Piao as Mao's heir.

The consistency with which the Marcyites identify Stalinism with a workers state was shown in the most striking way during the Hungarian uprising when they offered critical support to Khrushchev in using Soviet tanks and troops to crush the proletarian rebellion.

The Marcyites adopted the same position in relation to the current invasion and occupation of Czechoslovakia. They even went so far as to help the Kremlin in its efforts to find a propagandistic cover for crushing the upsurge that was pointing in the direction of a political revolution in Czechoslovakia.

Later in the SWP, we had the sad case of Arne Swabeck, one of the founders of the American Trotskyist movement, who proceeded from the theoretical position that only a revolutionary Marxist party can lead a successful revolution. Inasmuch as the Chinese Revolution was successful, he concluded that the Chinese Communist Party must have been a revolutionary Marxist party, and he ended up as a Maoist.

Juan Posadas followed a similar line of thinking

but with an odd twist. Because of Mao's supposed receptivity to genuine Marxism, Posadas came to believe that Mao derived his finest thought from reading the speeches and writings of J. Posadas. Just how this was accomplished was never made quite clear. Perhaps Posadas believed that Mao had set up a Latin-American Bureau in Peking that occupied itself with translating Juanposadas Thought into Chinese ideograms so that Chairman Mao could imbibe at this fountain.

The identification of Stalinism with a workers state took a different and perhaps still more remarkable twist in the thinking of Gerry Healy. He maintains that there are two, and only two, roads to a workers state—either under the leadership of a Trotskyist party or under the leadership of a Stalinist party.

Thus in the case of Cuba, Gerry Healy refuses to recognize the existence of a workers state because the revolution was headed by neither a Trotskyist party nor a Stalinist party.

Wohlforth lays it on the line

If you wish proof of this aberration, it has conveniently been made available in the most recent issue of the *Bulletin* (August 26). On pages S-5 and S-6, Tim Wohlforth, who seems to have displaced Cliff Slaughter as Healy's chief apologist, explains this remarkable theory.

In Eastern Europe, he says,

> The very process of expropriation of capital in these countries was accompanied by a process of the creation of this workers' bureaucracy through the taking over of the government by a workers' party, the Communist Party, and the purging of the government of all forces unreliable to the tasks this party had to carry out—some positive social tasks as well as reactionary tasks.

Wohlforth continues:

> The Castro government is in no sense a workers' bureaucracy. In fact Castro has carried out a series of purges against even Stalinist elements within his government—as illustrated by the two Escalante affairs—and maintains complete control in the hands of the petty-bourgeois nationalist forces who came to power with him.

Then Wohlforth gets down to the nitty gritty:

> In Cuba, and only in Cuba, the nationalizations were not accompanied by the emergence of a government controlled by the Stalinists.

We hardly need any further enlightenment from this Healyite theoretician. His position is that if the process that actually occurred in Cuba had been led by a Stalinist, say Blas Roca or Aníbal Escalante, then the Healyites would have at once agreed that a workers state had been established. If Blas Roca or Aníbal Escalante had purged Fidel Castro and Che Guevara this would have been proof positive.

But since the Stalinists in Cuba were outflanked and bypassed from the left by fresh revolutionary forces, the Healyites find it incompatible with their dogma to admit that a workers state has been established there.

It is this reactionary theory that has led the Healyites, out of concern for consistency, to commit such abominations as to call Castro another "Batista," to offer critical support to Cuban Stalinism when Castro became alarmed at the growth of bureaucratism, and to speculate, as they did openly in their press after Che Guevara left Havana in 1965 for another "assignment," that Castro had murdered his comrade-in-arms.

Now for the icing on the cake. The Healyites make a great show in their press of alertness to the danger of succumbing to Stalinism. However, they have not set a very good example in practice. Besides succumbing to the temptations of Stalinism in Cuba, they succumbed in China.

During the "cultural revolution," the *Newsletter* suddenly blossomed with rave articles about Mao's Red Guards. It was quite a sight to see the great red banner of Maoism lifted high in the *Newsletter*. This lasted but a short time. Praise for Mao's Red Guards vanished as abruptly as it had appeared. For the past two years, the *Newsletter* has hardly mentioned the "cultural revolution."

What happened? No explanation was ever offered. I suppose that the headquarters gang managed to get the ailing author of the articles back into a straitjacket and that was that. It never occurred to them that he was only acting in strict consistency with Gerryhealy Thought.

Four main results of war

The world Trotskyist movement never landed in such blind alleys as the ones in which Marcy, Swabeck, Posadas, and Healy are now to be found. At the same time, I think it is just to say that we have not yet achieved a fully satisfactory unified theory.

Perhaps we are now in position to accomplish this. With good fortune, this may be one of the outcomes of the current discussion.

The method we should follow is that of historical materialism—not the "objectivist" theory, the "accident" theory, or "eclectic dualism." Studies pursued in accordance with the method of historical materialism are the most likely to bring solid results. So let us look at the process that brought into the world the second generation of workers states.

World War II had four main consequences: (1) the victory of the Soviet Union; (2) the weakening of world capitalism as a whole; (3) the resulting temporary strengthening of Stalinism; (4) an upsurge of revolutionary struggles in both the imperialist centers and the colonial areas.

These four results shaped the course of history for some time, above all the advance of the world revolution.

Eastern Europe

In the case of the East European countries that were occupied by the Soviet armies as they moved toward Berlin, the overturn of capitalism in those areas was explainable as a direct consequence of the victory of the Soviet Union over German imperialism.

The armed struggle was carried on by the Soviet armies and the resistance movement operating in conjunction with them. The capitalist governments collapsed as the Soviet troops advanced. They were replaced by governments in which Moscow, standing behind local Stalinist parties, exercised power.

For a time the Kremlin retained the capitalist structures in Eastern Europe, evidently as bargaining pieces in trying to reach some kind of world settlement with Western imperialism.

When this bid was turned down and Washington opened up the Cold War, Stalin responded by destroying the capitalist structures in the countries occupied by the Soviet armies.

Imperialism was too weak to block the overturns. Naturally, there was a great hue and cry. But no capitalist country in Europe had the armed forces required to push back the Soviet armies. Even the U.S. armed forces were disintegrating.

The economic forms that replaced the capitalist structure in Eastern Europe were patterned on the economic forms in the Soviet Union. The structure of the state was likewise based on the Soviet model.

The proletarian element in these newly set up workers states clearly derived from the economic forms that were "structurally assimilated," to use the descriptive phrase applied by the comrades in Europe at the time.

The source of the reactionary Stalinist element, that is, the totalitarian political forms, was the Kremlin bureaucracy, the parasitic ruling caste which was keenly alert to the need to set up a replica of its own formation in these satellite states. Possible sources of political dissidence were handled with frame-up trials and purges.

We, of course, favored the overturns in Eastern Europe although we were absolutely opposed to the means used. To us, the overturns constituted fresh proof that the October Revolution was still alive. Stalin had not succeeded in destroying the foundations of the workers state. Despite himself he had had to export Soviet property forms, if only as a defensive measure against imperialism.

At the same time we were fully aware that the basic policy of the Soviet bureaucracy was "peaceful coexistence" with imperialism and that in accordance with this policy Stalin had once again, during these very same years, betrayed the big revolutionary upsurges in Italy, France, and elsewhere.

Yugoslavia

Let us now consider Yugoslavia. Here again, the Soviet victory was the decisive element. This victory served to inspire the Yugoslav people who had already become armed during their struggle against the German occupation.

The Yugoslav Communist Party had played an auxiliary role in the Soviet military defense by organizing the resistance in Yugoslavia against the German occupation and by pinning down German forces through guerrilla warfare. The armed struggle in Yugoslavia was thus linked to the victories of the Soviet armies.

But the Soviet armies did not play a direct role in Yugoslavia as they did in countries like Bulgaria.

British and American imperialism sought to counter the government set up by Tito by bolstering the forces favoring the monarchy. However, they were too weak to succeed in this, even with the connivance of Stalin. The armed forces under Tito smashed the counterrevolution and became the sole real governing power in Yugoslavia.

This government, in turn, took the steps ending capitalism in Yugoslavia. The economic forms that replaced capitalism were modeled on those in the Soviet Union.

In the political arena, Tito, in true Stalinist style, crushed all dissidence or what might appear to be a potential source of dissidence from the left.

Although the independent role played by the Yugoslav Communist Party under Tito was much greater than that of the Communist parties in countries like Rumania and Czechoslovakia under the Soviet occupation, the basic pattern of the process that ended in the establishment of a deformed workers state in Yugoslavia was the same.

Let us turn now to China. The main condition for the peculiar form which the revolutionary process took there was the same as in the East European countries and Yugoslavia—the victory of the Soviet Union in World War II.

The two other conditions following from this one were likewise the same—the weakening of world capitalism and the temporary strengthening of Stalinism.

As for the revolutionary upsurge touched off by the course of the war and its outcome, this occurred on the colossal scale of the most populous country on earth.

As in Eastern Europe and Yugoslavia, the Soviet armies played a certain role by their proximity in the final stage of the war against the Japanese imperialist aggression, but to a lesser degree than in the European theater.

There were other differences, some of them of an unexpected nature.

China's historic pattern

I should like to suggest that the first of these was the strong resemblance of the opening phases of the third Chinese revolution to the revolutions of former times in Chinese history.

The earlier revolutions followed a cyclical pattern. When the exploiting classes in China reached the point of exerting intolerable oppression on the masses, the entire economic system tended to break down. The remarkable canal system upon which so much of Chinese agriculture depended fell into disrepair. It became increasingly difficult to feed the population. Famines began to occur. The central authority became increasingly hated. Finally, the peasantry, goaded to desperation, began to link up, and, more importantly, to organize for battle.

A phase of armed struggle opened, with its guerrillas, focal centers, and peasant armies. Eventually these armies conquered, and a new government, headed by the leaders of the insurgent armies, came into power.

The new government at once went to work to repair the ravages of the civil war, to reduce the exploitation of the peasants, to divide up the land at the expense of the former landlords. The canal system was rehabilitated and extended, once again assuring a dependable supply of food for the population.

The army hierarchy that constituted the new government naturally soon displayed concern for its own comfort, ease, and even modest luxuries. The hierarchy developed into a privileged bureaucracy. The land became concentrated once again in fewer and fewer hands and the new dynasty came to represent the new landlords. The oppression of the peasantry became worse and worse and the system began to break down once again.

The most interesting part of this ancient pattern is the way the peasants succeeded in uniting and building armies imbued with a central political purpose and capable of smashing the old regime and putting a new and better one in power.

A comparison of this phase of the old pattern with the first stages of the third Chinese revolution would, in my opinion, prove highly instructive.

For one thing, it should help counteract the compulsion felt by our movement for so long to find some kind of proletarian quality in the Chinese peasants to account for their remarkable capacity to create a peasant army imbued with revolutionary political aims.

In any case it would make a very good research project for some young Trotskyist theoretician. So much for that point. We come now to more important items.

New world context

Upon achieving their victory in 1949, the peasant armies of the third Chinese revolution were, of course, confronted by a quite different world from the one their forefathers faced.

First of all, the class nature of the enemy was not the same. In addition they found themselves up against the invading armies of Japanese imperialism, and a little later a fresh threat of invasion from Chiang Kai-shek's American backers, who launched the Korean War and carried their aggression up to the Yalu River.

On top of this, the Chinese peasants established their government in the age of nuclear power, television, jet engines, intercontinental missiles, space rocketry. It was a world dominated by two superpowers, the United States and the Soviet Union—the one tied in with Chiang Kai-shek and standing behind the armies of President Truman and General MacArthur, the other associated with the common struggle against Japan, economic planning, and the immense achievements since 1917 that had lifted Russia out of abysmal backwardness.

Thus the consequence of the victory could not be a mere repetition of China's ancient cycle of revolution and counterrevolution, hinging on the status of agriculture and the private property relations associated with it.

The victory won by the Chinese peasant armies was bound to be shaped by the international context in which it occurred.

Role of armed struggle

The capacity displayed by the Chinese peasants to mobilize themselves in the absence of leadership from the Chinese proletariat gave the armed struggle in China extraordinary force and staying power. Here, too, a special study might provide our movement with very valuable new material.

In checking back in the documents written when China first came up for intensive discussion in our movement, I was struck by the absence of consideration of the role played by the sustained armed struggle.

For instance, in the May 1952 resolution of the International Executive Committee of the Fourth International, which was published in the July–August 1952 issue of *Fourth International,* there is a list of the ways in which the Soviet bureaucracy sought to block the Chinese Revolution from developing into a proletarian revolution. Among the ways, we are told, was the following: "By the pressure exerted upon the Chinese CP to maintain the tactic of guerrilla warfare, and not to attack the big cities."

This could be taken to mean that Stalin favored rural guerrilla warfare for a prolonged period, but was against urban guerrilla war or, more likely, was against the deployment of the peasant armies to take the big cities when that stage of the guerrilla struggle was reached. At one time, of course, he inspired an opposite course—of attacking cities prematurely.

The resolution contains nothing more than this about the import of the armed struggle in the Chinese Revolution.

It is obvious, I think, that if the 1952 resolution had been written in the light of the Cuban experience, or even in the light of the Algerian experience, that a quite different approach would have been taken on this question.

The truth of it is that quite large forces were involved in the armed struggle even in the early stages. In his successive campaigns to liquidate the so-called soviets set up by Mao in Kiangsi in the early thirties, Chiang Kai-shek utilized armies numbering in the hundreds of thousands.

Three of these massive campaigns were defeated by the revolutionary peasant armies, and in 1931 Mao proclaimed a "Chinese Soviet Republic" in this region. It took two more huge campaigns to dislodge this government and compel Mao to begin the Long March in 1934.

A new base was established in Shensi. For a time the armed struggle against the Chiang Kai-shek government was given up in favor of an alliance with the Chinese bourgeoisie and its political representatives. However, the armed struggle continued for a number of years against the Japanese imperialist forces; and in this struggle the revolutionary peasant armies gained in experience and above all in size until they numbered in the millions. We can well appreciate the pressure they exerted to carry the struggle through to the end.

These armies were highly organized—as was required to defeat the enemy—and thus gave rise to a structure of command with vast ramifications. It would be a great contribution to our knowledge if we could know the absolute size of this network, its relations with other mass organizations, and what changes may have occurred in its outlook after the victory.

Workers and peasants government

The role of the peasant guerrillas and the peasant armies is intimately linked to the role played by the successive governments that were set up in the bases controlled by them.

According to Mao, the government of the Chinese Soviet Republic in Kiangsi had 9,000,000 persons under its rule. In relation to China as a whole that was only a modest number. Just the same it was greater than the population of Cuba today.

In 1937, Mao reduced the "Chinese Soviet Republic" to a "regional authority" covering Shensi, Kansu and Ninghsia. The number of subjects was probably a couple of million at most—say a population something like that in Albania today. Nevertheless from this base, Mao's regional government expanded on a big scale during the war against the Japanese imperialist invaders. Similar regional governments were set up until a hundred million persons or so came under the rule of "Red" or "People's" China.

Thus when the workers and peasants government was established in Peking in 1949, long years of experience in wielding government power had already been accumulated by the apparatus under Mao's command.

How to handle a huge military structure, undertake public works, collect taxes, apply oppressive measures, grant concessions, judge which political currents should be ruthlessly stamped out (such as the Trotskyists) and which should be brought into a "coalition" (such as the "democratic-minded" capitalists and their political parties); how to conduct a foreign policy in keeping with the interests of the apparatus—in short, the whole business of running governmental affairs was already old stuff for the Maoist team.

Thus the workers and peasants government headed by Mao that was established in 1949 had a long background of experience that was invaluable in the task of getting things going and rehabilitating the country after the destruction, dislocations, and havoc China had suffered under Chiang Kai-shek and the imperialist armies of Japan.

In the early years not much attention was paid to the sector of China governed by Mao. Thus it is difficult to form an accurate picture of the way Mao ruled in the period before moving to Peking in 1949 and establishing his fourth capital there. (Juichin, Pao An, Yenan, Peking.)

What kind of justice prevailed under Mao during these decisive years? Was it balanced and fair? Was democracy practiced? Did even a semblance of democracy exist? Or did Mao follow the practices he admired so much in Stalin?

I think that we can make a fairly good guess.

When the peasant armies finally took the cities, they not only put Chiang Kai-shek and his forces to flight, they suppressed every move of the proletariat to engage as an independent force in the revolutionary upsurge. In following this policy, Mao was not initiating something new, he was continuing what he had practiced for years. Stalinism was congenital in the new regime.

Stalinism, a temporary phenomenon

Perhaps this is the place to consider Trotsky's thesis that Stalinism was a temporary phenomenon, doomed to disappear with the advance of the revolution. This is absolutely correct on a historic scale. Trotsky based it on the consideration that with the success of the proletarian revolution in one or more advanced capitalist countries, the standard of living could be raised so rapidly as to destroy Stalinism economically, since Stalinism arose as a product of a backward economy in a country subjected to extreme isolation and pressure by world capitalism.

But Trotsky did not speculate on what might occur if the proletarian revolution in the advanced capitalist countries was delayed for several more decades while the revolution conquered in areas still more backward than Czarist Russia.

We have seen what happens in this case. It is a matter of history. Stalinism is temporarily strengthened and its death agony is prolonged.

Trotsky's thesis nevertheless caused many comrades to scan Maoism with the hope that it might prove to be anti-Stalinist and thus provide early confirmation of Trotsky's prognosis on the historic fate of Stalinism.

Mao's policy in Indonesia and his course in the "cultural revolution" have shown how misplaced these hopes were.

Birth of Chinese workers state

Let us continue with our analysis.

The workers and peasants government that began wielding power in Peking in 1949 was decisive in another respect in shaping the ultimate outcome of the Chinese Revolution.

It was this government that finally destroyed the capitalist state and established a workers state in China. This took place despite Mao's "New Democracy" program of maintaining capitalism for a prolonged period. The tasks faced by the new regime, particularly when they were compounded by the aggression of American imperialism in Korea, were of such order that they could be met only through economic forms that are socialist in principle.

The establishment of a workers state in China offered the most striking testimony as to the validity of the basic premise in Trotsky's theory of the permanent revolution; namely, the tendency of revolutions in the backward countries to transcend the bourgeois-democratic phase and turn into socialist revolutions. Our movement has correctly placed a great deal of stress on this; it is not necessary for me to repeat it here.

What I should like to call special attention to is the link in the revolutionary process through which this qualitative leap was made possible—the workers and peasants government.

From the theoretical point of view this is the item of greatest interest, for it was this government that set up the economic forms modeled on those existing in the Soviet Union, repeating what had happened in Eastern Europe and Yugoslavia.

The possibility of workers and peasants governments coming to power had been visualized by the Communist International at the Fourth Congress in 1922. But the Bolsheviks held that such governments, set up by petty-bourgeois parties could not be characterized as proletarian dictatorships, that is, workers states.

The Bolsheviks were firmly convinced that petty-bourgeois parties, even though they went so far as to establish a workers and peasants government, could never move forward to establish a workers state. Only a revolutionary Communist party, rooted in the working class on a mass scale so as to be able to lead it into action, could do that.

The experience in China showed that in at least one case history had decreed otherwise.

This came on top of the experience in Yugoslavia and in Eastern Europe where it can be argued that the implications were not so clear cut because of the role played by the Soviet armies, the catastrophe suffered by German imperialism, and the revolutionary crisis suffered by the other capitalist powers in Europe.

It was precisely because of the adjustment that would be required in the hypothesis advanced by the Fourth Congress of the Communist International that our party moved so cautiously and sought to explore every possible alternative before it agreed to recognize that a workers state had been established in China. We take a very serious attitude toward theory.

The thoroughness with which we sought to examine the consequences of the Chinese experience served as good preparation for what happened in Cuba some ten years after the Chinese victory. We were able to follow the pattern of events in Cuba with ease.

The most gratifying aspect of this from the standpoint of theory was that the pattern of the Cuban Revolution decisively confirmed the principal conclusions we had reached with regard to China.

Cuba and Algeria

The key item in Cuba was the workers and peasants government established in 1959 by a petty-bourgeois political force, the July 26 Movement.

As in the case of China, this new Cuban government, which had been brought to power through a hard-fought armed struggle and a revolution of the most deep-going and popular character, could not meet the giant tasks it faced, particularly in face of the violent reaction of U.S. imperialism, without toppling the capitalist structure and establishing economic forms that were socialist in principle.

Once again, these were modeled by and large on those in the Soviet Union. Even more than in the case of China, the very possibility of a workers state in Cuba of any durability hinged on the existence of the Soviet Union. The appearance of a viable workers state in Cuba was thus a consequence, in the final analysis, of the victory of the Soviet Union in World War II.

The pattern was similarly visible in the Algerian Revolution. In this instance, however, no workers state was established. Instead the workers and peasants government was brought down by a military coup d'état in June 1965 after some three years in power.

This was proof that the establishment of a workers and peasants government does not automatically guarantee the subsequent establishment of a workers state.

In the case of Cuba, a significant new development was to be observed. The leadership that came to power, while it was petty-bourgeois, was not trained in the school of Stalinism. It stood to the left of the Cuban Communist Party.

The importance of this cannot be overemphasized. The team headed by Fidel Castro and Che Guevara constituted the first contingent of a new generation of revolutionists that cannot be brainwashed by either Moscow or Peking.

Trend toward classic norm

On the broad scale of the post–World War II period, this constitutes a watershed.

The deformation of the revolutionary process in Eastern Europe, in Yugoslavia, in China, in North Korea and North Vietnam was a resultant of the revolutionary upsurge following World War II coupled with the temporary strengthening of Stalinism.

The expansion of Stalinism, however, intensified its internal contradictions and this led to a series of crises that finally culminated in the Sino-Soviet conflict and the spread of "polycentrism." Stalinism has thus been greatly weakened. Even in its Maoist form, Stalinism now faces an increasingly dim future.

On the other hand, the establishment of a series of workers states as the consequence of successful revolutions has greatly strengthened the world revolution and its perspectives.

This means a growing tendency internationally toward a revolutionary pattern that comes much closer to the classic norm in which the proletariat moves into the foreground. Evidence of this is to be seen in the shifting of the axis of revolutionary struggles in the backward countries from the countryside to the cities. The events in France in May–June 1968 showed what explosive potential now exists in the imperialist centers of the West. The ghetto uprisings in the United States and the upsurge among the student youth internationally have offered further corroboration of the trend.

We can conclude from this that the next revolutionary victory, wherever it comes, will in all likelihood go even further than the Cuban Revolution in departing from the deformation imposed by the pernicious heritage of Stalinism. The Leninist norm, calling for construction of a fully conscious revolutionary-socialist combat party, will acquire full force and validity as revolutionary situations develop in the strongholds of world capitalism.

Consequences

What are the main consequences of viewing the Chinese Revolution along the lines I have indicated so far as the current discussion is concerned?

First of all, I would say that it is much easier to see the role played by the peasantry and its petty-bourgeois leadership. We can call them what they are, *petty-bourgeois*, without seeking to conjure away this fact or to ameliorate it by speculating that after all these forces must have been proletarian in some shape or fashion, otherwise the peasantry and the Stalinized Communist Party could not have played the role they did.

Secondly, we can see much more easily how a proletarian element did finally come into play in the Chinese Revolution through the governmental power that established economic forms modeled on those of the Soviet Union.

Thirdly, we can more easily see the continuous thread of Stalinism in China from the very beginning up to the current stage marked by the crisis and fierce factional struggle of the "cultural revolution." It is not necessary to look for periods in which Stalinism presumably vanished—only to reappear. We eliminate this awkward hypothesis which would require us to explain how Stalinism in China could have died in the flames of a peasant upheaval only to arise again from the ashes of the "great proletarian cultural revolution."

Fourthly, we can much more easily grasp the origins of the bureaucracy in China, how it was shaped by Stalinism as it came into being, and what a substantial element this bureaucracy actually is in the Chinese social and political scene.

Fifthly, we are in a better position to understand the interrelationship between Mao's domestic and foreign policies, and particularly in the case of his foreign policy to see how its basic design is to safeguard and advance the position of the bureaucratic ruling caste and why this gives his foreign policy its nationalistic "peaceful coexistence" characteristics and its capacity to alternate between rank opportunism and adventuristic ultraleftism. It becomes easier to see the true origin of Mao's foreign policy and to avoid the error of mistaking the *resultant* of the clash between Peking's policy and the contending policies of other countries with what Mao seeks to achieve.

Sixthly, by considering the pattern of the Chinese Revolution in conjunction with the patterns in Eastern Europe, Yugoslavia, Cuba, Algeria, we can much more readily appreciate the limitations of the lessons to be drawn. It is easier to avoid unwarranted and incorrect extrapolations that could prove very misleading and dangerous.

In mentioning these consequences, I should like to stress that they are derivative. They follow from viewing the Chinese Revolution in the way I have suggested.

What is most important, of course, is to weigh the validity of this analysis of the pattern of the Chinese Revolution and its connection with the patterns in Eastern Europe, Yugoslavia, Cuba, and Algeria.

In any case, as the discussion develops internationally on this subject, the most fruitful contributions may well be those that seek to fill in the extensive gaps that still exist in our knowledge of some of the phases of the Chinese Revolution that are of the greatest interest from the standpoint of theory.

State capitalism

Postscript:

Because of time limitations it was not possible for me to do more at the convention than barely refer during my summary to a point that should be considered logically in conjunction with the question of the degenerated or deformed workers states and their relationship to Stalinism. This is the peculiar state structures of countries like Egypt and Burma.

As is well known, in these countries the government has taken over the bulk of the means of production with the exception of agriculture.

The nationalizations are so extensive, in fact, that quantitatively the situation appears comparable to what exists in the workers states. As a result it is tempting to equate them with workers states; and this has been done—incorrectly so—by various currents.

One procedure of those who make this error is to call them workers states. Another is to call them state capitalist; but—still equating them with workers states—to call countries like the Soviet Union and China "state capitalist."

The essential difference between states like Egypt and genuine workers states is to be found in their different origin. In every instance, the workers states, whether deformed or otherwise, have emerged as products of revolutions. Through armed struggle, through upheavals involving the masses on an immense scale, the people have overthrown their capitalist oppressors, displacing them from power in the most thoroughgoing way.

In countries like Egypt, upheavals on this scale have not occurred. The usual pattern is that a sector of the officer caste takes over, generally through a coup d'état, occasionally ratified through partial mobilization of the masses, who, of course, are in favor of ousting the old regime.

The new government is fearful of the masses. One of the first things it does is to block the masses from mobilizing, at least in a massive revolutionary way. The new government aims at giving capitalism a new lease on life after a period in incubation under auspices of the state apparatus.

The officialdom is thoroughly aware of the ultimate perspective, and conducts itself accordingly. How the state machinery is used to spawn millionaires was graphically demonstrated in Mexico.

It is obvious that the qualitative nature of nationalizations is determined by whether they originate in a thoroughgoing revolutionary struggle or in measures undertaken by a sector of the officer caste or their political representatives, who may even have in mind forestalling a popular revolution by setting up a simulacrum of a workers state. This phenomenon can be quite correctly placed under the general heading of state capitalism.

What is demonstrated by the extensive nationalizations in countries like Egypt—and the less extensive ones in Mexico and elsewhere in Latin America—is the enormous pressure being exerted on a world scale to bring capitalism to a close and to move into the epoch of socialism. Private capitalism has become so antiquated, so outdated, that capitalist governments everywhere are compelled to intervene more and more extensively in the very management of industry if they hope to prolong the death agony of the system a bit longer.

The growth of state capitalism also testifies to the depth of the crisis in revolutionary leadership observable on an international scale. Prime responsibility for this lies with Stalinism.

The overhead cost of the many betrayals of the most promising revolutionary openings, from Germany in the early thirties to Indonesia three decades later, can be measured, among other ways, by the growth of statism, the direct intervention of the capitalist state in the economic system.

The importance of the occurrence of a *revolution*, as one of the criteria in determining that a workers state has come into existence is very clear in the case of Cuba.

Because they do not recognize this criterion, the Healyites refuse to acknowledge that a workers state exists in Cuba. They lump Cuba with Egypt, Burma, Syria, and so on.

They are inconsistent in not placing China and Yugoslavia in the same category. They seek to avoid this inconsistency by making the existence of *Stalinism* the decisive criterion. This shows that in the final analysis they are incapable of distinguishing between revolution and counterrevolution.

The qualitative difference that a revolution makes in nationalizations is evident in the difference in durability of the takeovers in countries where a revolution has occurred and countries where it has not occurred.

This is because of the fact that the old ruling class is smashed in the one instance and only temporarily displaced in the other while the state structure is used to rejuvenate the system. The marked difference in popular consciousness is likewise of prime importance.

Cuba and Burma offer striking examples of these differences.

A comparative study along these lines would undoubtedly prove highly instructive.

5. An exchange of letters between Joseph Hansen and Bob Chester

The following is a previously unpublished exchange of letters between Joseph Hansen and Bob Chester following the 1969 convention of the Socialist Workers Party. Bob Chester is an advisory member of the National Committee of the Socialist Workers Party.

NOTE ON HANSEN-CHESTER CORRESPONDENCE
by Bob Chester

This correspondence began as a partial misunderstanding of Joe Hansen's report to the 1969 convention (*Internal Information Bulletin* No. 4 in 1969), a misunderstanding that was cleared up in the course of the interchange. Joe viewed the formation of a workers and peasants government with the victory of Mao as a special case, and not as part of a pattern that would have designated workers and peasants governments in Yugoslavia and the buffer zone with the end of World War II, and in Cuba in January 1959.

There were a number of theoretical questions dealing with this topic that I felt needed clarification, and I utilized this opportunity to raise them. While the interchange has been in hiatus for the last few years, both Joe and I feel that the discussion is still continuing.

There is no doubt that the topic is important for the theoretical arsenal of our movement. It is a fruitful area for study and research, to which many comrades can make contributions.

AUGUST 26, 1973

LETTER FROM BOB CHESTER TO JOSEPH HANSEN

December 13, 1969

Dear Joe,

I want to raise a question on your report to the convention, "The Origin of the Differences on China," printed in Bulletin No. 4. While I consider the report as a whole an excellent one and would have supported it if I were at the convention, I am sure that I would have taken exception to the conclusions you presented on workers and peasants governments. [The relevant portions of this report are reprinted in this collection.]

As far as I know this is the first time we have claimed that Yugoslavia and the buffer countries had workers and peasants governments beginning with the defeat of the Nazis in 1945; that China had a workers and peasants government with the Mao victory in 1949; and that Cuba had a workers and peasants government with the victory of Jan. 1, 1959. I do not remember it being included in our resolutions covering these events and I believe it adds something new to our theory of the transformation of bourgeois states into workers states in colonial and semicolonial countries.

Previously we had concluded that what had been set up in the East European countries were coalition governments of native Stalinists, direct agents of Moscow, together with peasant, social democratic, and whatever capitalist elements they could find. The Red Army controlled and guided their operation. The Soviet Union plundered these countries of many basic factories, let capitalism operate on a national level, even set up joint stock companies with them, and paid little attention to the needs and wishes of the workers. These governments played a repressive rather than progressive role. Could these be considered as workers and peasants governments independent of the bourgeoisie? I think not. Even when the transition to a workers state took place as a reaction to the Marshall Plan, it was done on a controlled basis under the direct aegis of the Soviet bureaucracy. We termed this process "structural assimilation," and the result deformed workers states. Would you characterize the governments that effected these changes workers and peasants governments? If you do you would have to qualify them even further to account for the fact that they were acting as agents of the Soviet bureaucracy.

In the country having the most advanced mass participation in the revolutionary process, Yugoslavia, I do not think the Tito-Subasic government could be classed as a workers and peasants government. Even though it was short lived it was essentially a coalition government of Stalinists and capitalists set up under the pressure of the imperialists and Moscow. It is true that the government did not last long, that the bourgeois elements found little room to operate, and that with the failure of the coalition the Tito regime swung sharply left. From that point on the designation of workers and peasants government might apply.

In Cuba, the initial government set up with Urrutia as president could only be characterized as a coalition government, even though its program gave promise of more radical change. The institution of agrarian reform brought this government into crisis, ending with the ousting of Urrutia in the fall of 1959. The Draft Theses of Dec. 23, 1960 under point 7 begins with the statement, "The fact that Cuba *now* had a Workers and Farmers government. . . ." (my emphasis) reinforces the thinking that it became such a government with the expulsion of the capitalist wing.

In China, as your report details, Mao came to power at the head of a peasant army and took over the cities with the conscious policy of preventing the working class from playing any significant role in the revolution. They brought native capitalists into the government and announced a policy of peaceful and friendly relations with capitalist governments, including the United States. Land reform, which had been a feature of the pre-victory period, was curtailed and the Peoples Democracy they visualized was one that would continue for a prolonged period. It was the Korean events with the threat of U.S. invasion that spurred the leftward shift that ended in the formation of the deformed workers state. You raise the question of how we would designate the Mao regime in the years before the 1949 victory and pose the possibility of a workers and peasants government in the years before that victory. If that were so it seems to me that a shift in the manner of rule occurred with the national government set up in 1949.

It is true that our concept of the type of government that existed in the transition period has never been fully developed. There has always been a period during the leftward shift, before we could designate these states as workers states (deformed or otherwise) with workers governments at their head, that we used the term "Workers and Peasants Governments." Even then we never clearly established what the distinctive characteristics of these governments were nor did we identify them as the necessary "link in the revolutionary process" that established these workers states. It seems to me that this is precisely the problem we have to solve.

When a revolution takes place in a colonial or semicolonial country with the active participation of the masses in support of a leadership that can be either worker, peasant or middle class, can we immediately designate this as a workers and peasants government? What are the characteristics that make it "worker and peasant government" rather than radical bourgeois or peasant? What would be the points of qualitative change of one to the other? Above all, what are the dynamics of a worker and peasant regime that make it the "link in the revolutionary process?" I know that these questions have not been answered to my satisfaction.

Neither can I see how the theses and discussions at the Fourth Congress of the C.I. are really applicable here. They deal essentially with the tactics used by a revolutionary party during a period of crisis when it does not yet have hegemony over the working class. The purpose of these tactics, which are basically that of critical support and the united front, are to force the reformist governments leftward, expose the reformist leaders and speed the process of radicalization of the working class and its allies. The objective was the formation of a workers and peasants government under the leadership of the revolutionary party that would in essence be the dictatorship of the proletariat.

It is true that the Congress listed four different types of workers or workers and peasants governments, and listed them under these classifications in order to set their tactical orientation to each. It also pointed to the fact that "liberal workers governments" such as the British Labour Party and "social democratic workers governments" as in Germany were in essence "coalition governments of the bourgeoisie and anti-revolutionary labor leaders" who would have to be overthrown in the course of the struggle.

In the light of the Theses of the Fourth Congress how could you possibly explain a petty bourgeois leadership that emerges out of the national struggle and *as a body* with comparatively few defections goes through the transition to a workers state? I see this as a verification of the theory of permanent revolution and not of the Theses of the Fourth Congress. If they can be classed as workers and peasants governments, then they are new and special types which require independent analysis.

I have tried to think this problem through and, after generalizing the whole experience on the question, have come up with some different answers. I would like to get your reaction to them.

It seems to me that the solution lies in a closer examination of the national liberation struggles under the special set of circumstances that have existed from the end of World War II. They include the considerable weakening of imperialism on a world scale; the enhanced strength and prestige of the Soviet Union; the great weight and power of the colonial struggles for liberation; the reduced size, strength and loss of confidence of the native capitalists. These were bolstered in former periods by the weight of the compradore bourgeoisie, but these sections now flee at the early stage of struggle leaving the native capitalists even weaker. Add to this the chronic crisis of the peasantry.

A revolutionary movement rising out of the national struggle, even under middle class leadership, sees imperialism as its main enemy and also sees a counterbalance to it—the attractive power of the Soviet Union and the other workers states. The movement feels that imperialism no longer has such overwhelming power that it cannot be opposed or defied. There is now room for maneuver. It is no accident that there has emerged a "third world" section, the so-called neutrals, that play both sides in an attempt to gain some advantages for themselves.

The national character of the movement gives the leadership an added advantage, in that it can gain support of workers and peasants as well as the middle class and some section of the capitalists in its fight against imperialism. If there was a conscious revolutionary party on the scene this "national unity" would not exist but would separate into sharply contending wings of the class struggle. The process would then take a different road, following more closely the pattern of struggle laid out by Trotsky, where the capitalists and their reformist supporters would be progressively isolated and the workers with their peasant allies would move toward power, to a workers and peasants government or directly toward a dictatorship of the proletariat. With the absence or failure of a revolutionary party to rise to the situation a petty bourgeois leadership can get the support of diverse elements and come to power on a limited, short term program meeting the new situations in its typical empirical fashion.

The attitude of the imperialists is crucial. If it is hostile and adamantly opposes the leftward swing, especially nationalizations of "its" holdings, the revolution has the option of turning to the Soviet Union for aid. Where the leadership had Stalinist origins as in Yugoslavia, China, and Vietnam, this reaction would be on the order of an automatic reflex. In Cuba the turn to the Soviet Union went hand in hand with the sharpening of the struggle with Washington. If the imperialists adopt a more flexible attitude and make concessions in order to maintain some economic ties the process can be slowed down or even reversed. I think Algeria is an example of this. The lever France used was that of economic agreements, especially on the exploitation of Sahara oil.

Nationalization is a logical step for a backward country that must find the means of setting up enterprises for national survival or for trade on the world market. There is no other national source to finance them. Taking over the property of the huge imperialist monopolies is a natural starting point for national independence. The recent examples in Bolivia and Chile indicate how strong this pressure is even on bourgeois leaders friendly to imperialism. Where the masses participate in the revolutionary process nationalization is far more sweeping, especially where Soviet aid and advice become large factors in the nationalization process. Control of foreign trade and banking become natural logical steps as measures of defense if not as positive policies to defend the gains already achieved.

Thus the struggle, beginning at the level of national liberation, with the support of the masses moves on past the national level into the permanent revolution. What is essential for the process to develop into the workers state form is the maintenance of the pressures that started the revolution in the first place; a national revolutionary upsurge, a leadership responsive in some measure to the mass pressure, hostility to imperialism concretized in nationalizations, elimination of capitalist elements that oppose this process and the continued pressure of imperialism that prevents any stabilization and adaptation to a peaceful coexistence at some intermediate stage. With this also develops a socialist consciousness which has either been in the background of the movement or has been acquired in the course of the struggle.

Does a government that carries out these measures have to be a workers and peasants government? Could it not be carried out by a petty bourgeois government or even a national coalition of anti-imperialist forces, at least in the early stages? The experiences of the twenties and thirties indicated that when the middle class was caught between class pressures the majority invariably gravitated toward capitalism. With the relationships changing in the post World War II period it is more possible for sections of the middle class, when under the pressure of the mass movement, to gravitate toward the working class. This has apparently happened in a few special cases.

It is clear that the negative factors persist in this development. While they follow the main line of permanent revolution the transition is not thorough nor complete. They result in deformed or incompleted workers states and remain on the national level. Where they go beyond the national level, it is solely as a measure of national defense. While the leaderships have opposed or eliminated threats from the right they equally oppose tendencies from the left that try to move the struggle to the international level.

This is the main outline of my thinking on the problems posed by your report to the convention.

I admit that I have not thought through a number of theoretical and tactical problems raised by them. That is why I am posing them on a tentative basis. I believe they are important enough to be included in the general discussion that is now under way.

I am not raising these ideas as a necessary projection for the future, only as a generalization of what has happened. It is quite possible that we are entering a new stage that will not follow the previous pattern. The French events of 1968 are one sign of a change. There is also a new awareness by U.S. imperialism of its failure in the cases of China and Cuba to prevent the formation of hostile workers states, that might express itself in a shift in approach to new revolutionary movements. There is also a growth of revolutionary Marxist trends in some of the colonial countries that could sharply change the character of the national struggles. Any one of these factors can have a strong effect upon the type of revolutionary forces that emerge on the scene of colonial struggle.

I hope to get your views on my criticism of your convention report as well as on the other views I have raised.

Comradely,
Bob Chester

LETTER FROM JOSEPH HANSEN TO BOB CHESTER

July 26, 1970

Dear Bob,

First of all I want to express my appreciation for your patience in waiting such a long time for me to reply to your letter of last December 13. As I explained when I had a chance to talk with you about this, I wanted to go back and check particular items you had raised. I especially had in mind going in some detail into several of the overturns of capitalism that have occurred in circumstances other than under the leadership of a revolutionary-Marxist party. Unfortunately I have not been able to make time for this although it is certainly required if an adequate response is to be written to the many important questions you have raised. Finally I decided that further delay was simply impermissible and that in the absence of the research that ought to be done, I could write down my reactions to your letter. It would be easiest if I could just take your letter paragraph by paragraph. This is rather awkward, but how else can we proceed like a conversation? So get out your letter to refer to as I go along. To help out some, I will number the items and quote extensively from what you say.

1. As far as I know this is the first time we have claimed that Yugoslavia and the buffer countries had workers and peasants governments beginning with the defeat of the Nazis in 1945; that China had a workers and peasants government with the Mao victory in 1949; and that Cuba had a workers and peasants government with the victory of January 1, 1959. I do not remember it being included in our resolutions covering these events and I believe it adds something new to our theory of the transformation of bourgeois states into workers states in colonial and semicolonial countries.

In response to this I think it is true that our resolutions in general dealt only with the main question of the toppling of the capitalist state in those countries and its replacement by a workers state of one kind or another (generally "deformed"). Our resolutions did not go into the details of the process involving the transfer of power. As to the dates you indicate, I will not go into these here because, as I said, I have not been able to make time to dig into details. In the case of Cuba, however, I will make an exception. In the Winter 1961 issue of the *International Socialist Review* I wrote:

> On coming to power, the July 26 movement set up a coalition government that included well-known bourgeois democratic figures—and not in secondary posts. In retrospect these may have seemed middle-class decorations or mere camouflage hiding the real nature of the government. It is more accurate, I think, to view this government as corresponding to the political aims of the revolution as they were conceived at that time by its leaders.
>
> But such a government stood in contradiction to the demands of the insurgent masses and to the commitment of the July 26 movement to satisfy these demands. The Revolu-

tion urgently required far-reaching inroads on private property, including imperialist holdings. As Castro and his collaborators moved toward fulfillment of the agrarian reform they met with resistance from their partners in the coalition, a resistance that was considerably stiffened by support from Wall Street which viewed them as 'reasonable' elements in a regime packed with bearded 'wild men.'

As Huberman and Sweezy correctly observe, 'a sort of dual system government began to emerge.' The displacement of Felipe Pazos by Che Guevara in November 1959 marked a decisive shift and the resolution of the governmental crisis, whatever hang-overs from the coalition still remained. The government that now existed was qualitatively different from the coalition regime.

I then went on to develop the view that this was a "Workers and Farmers Government" and that this government initiated and carried out the measures that brought the workers state into being in Cuba "between August–October, 1960. . . ."

To continue with your letter:

> 2. Previously we had concluded that what had been set up in the East European countries were coalition governments of native Stalinists, direct agents of Moscow, together with peasant, social democrats, and whatever capitalist elements they could find.

As we have seen in the case of Cuba, the setting up of a *coalition government* does not exhaust the process. The question under examination requires an analysis in finer detail. We can understand what is involved if we ask, does the appearance of a *coalition* government open the possibility of a socialist overturn in the absence of a revolutionary-Marxist party? If so, what will most likely be the process by which such an overturn will occur?

I agree with your observations about the real power in Eastern Europe being exercised by the Red Army and that this was the decisive force in the overturns. However, I think you overlook an important link in the organization of local committees and indigenous governments. Some of the figures in these governments proved not to be "direct agents of Moscow." This was shown shortly thereafter by the extensive purges in Eastern Europe and the jailing and execution of various prominent leaders. I seem to recall Trotsky warning of such a possibility when he was discussing the Finnish events at the beginning of World War II, or perhaps it was the Polish events. In the light of the uprisings in later years in East Germany, Poland, Hungary, and the struggle in Czechoslovakia, it would be worth reexamining in detail the process by which capitalism was toppled in Eastern Europe to fix in a more precise way the role of the native Stalinists in distinction from the direct agents of Moscow. However, as I had to admit earlier, I couldn't make time for this.

> 3. We termed this process 'structural assimilation,' and the result deformed workers states.

The term "structural assimilation" was always somewhat puzzling to me.

When I was in Europe in 1962 I took up this question with the comrades who had first used the term. They said they meant something simpler than we had imagined in translating what they had written. "Structural assimilation" to them merely referred to the fact that the economic and state forms that had appeared in Eastern Europe were modeled on those of the Soviet Union. "Structural assimilation" thus occurred also in the case of Yugoslavia and China, likewise in Cuba, although to a lesser degree.

But the comrades in Europe did not follow the process in the finer detail that concerns us in the question of the role of workers and peasants governments under the conditions we have specified.

> 4. Would you characterize the governments that effected these changes workers and peasants governments?

The problem is one of substance. Did indigenous governments exist in these countries? If so, what role did they play in the transfer of power and the establishment of deformed workers states? Their role may not have been much; but evidently it was sufficient to lead Stalin to decapitate them—and at a rather early stage.

> 5. If you do you would have to qualify them even further to account for the fact that they were acting as agents of the Soviet bureaucracy.

I would agree to this if you in turn would agree that while being agents they were also at the very same time not agents, or at least had the potentiality of not being agents. The case of Tito is outstanding but the same holds for others like Rajk whom Stalin succeeded in liquidating.

> 6. In the country having the most advanced mass participation in the revolutionary process, Yugoslavia, I do not think the Tito-Subasic government could be classed as a workers and peasants government. Even though it was short lived it was essentially a coalition government of Stalinists and capitalists set up under the pressure of the imperialists and Moscow. It is true that the government did not last long, that the bourgeois elements found little room to operate, and that with the failure of the coalition the Tito regime swung sharply left. From that point on the designation of workers and peasants government might apply.

This is one of the items in your letter that I would have liked to check out in order to determine more specifically the points of qualitative change. Among the things of special interest: (a) Which wing was dominant in the coalition? (b) When the qualitative change occurred from a coalition government to a government so radical in nature that it was capable of destroying the capitalist state structure (and the capitalist economic forms) and establishing a workers state, then it would seem obvious that not only was the date important but also the nature of the new government.

This is precisely the key point under discussion. You say: "From that point on the designation of workers and peasants government might apply." With this sentence haven't you in essence conceded the case I have been arguing for? For if it "might apply" to Yugoslavia, why might it not also apply to the other cases? Once you have made such a concession in a *single* instance, it appears to me insuperably difficult from a methodological point of view to maintain that it be excluded in all *other* instances where comparable governments have similarly ended capitalism and established workers states.

But then why the hesitancy? Why "might apply" instead of "does apply"?

> 7. In Cuba, the initial government set up with Urrutia as president could only be characterized as a coalition government, even though its program gave promise of more radical change. The institution of agrarian reform brought this government into crisis, ending with the ousting of Urrutia in the fall of 1959. The Draft Theses of Dec. 23, 1960 under point 7 begins with the statement: 'The fact that Cuba *now* had a Workers and Farmers government. . . .' (my emphasis) reinforces the thinking that it became such a government with the expulsion of the capitalist wing.

I, of course, agree with your observations outside of the item as to the point of qualitative change and I would not argue much about that. The ouster of Urrutia could well be considered to have marked the point of qualitative change. At the time this occurred, however, I preferred to wait to see what the positive consequences of the negation might be. Caution was dictated, I thought, because of the absence of any declared anticapitalist and prosocialist program of the Castro wing. When Che Guevara was moved into a key position and then took charge of carrying through the changes that brought the first workers state into being in the Western hemisphere, that appeared to me to mark an unquestionable point of qualitative change as determined on the level of *action.*

> 8. In China, as your report details, Mao came to power at the head of a peasant army and took over the cities with the conscious policy of preventing the working class from playing any significant role in the revolution. They brought native capitalists into the government and announced a policy of peaceful

and friendly relations with capitalist governments, including the United States. Land reform, which had been a feature of the pre-victory period was curtailed and the Peoples Democracy they visualized was one that would continue for a prolonged period. It was the Korean events with the threat of U.S. invasion that spurred the leftward shift that ended in the formation of the deformed workers state. You raise the questions of how we would designate the Mao regime in the years before the 1949 victory and pose the possibility of a workers and peasants government in the years before that victory. If that were so it seems to me that a shift in the manner of rule occurred with the national government set up in 1949.

I do not disagree with your general description. The question of a "workers and peasants government" falls *within* this general description. For instance, you say: "It was the Korean events with the threat of U.S. invasion that spurred the leftward shift that ended in the formation of the deformed workers state." The question I raise is "leftward shift" of *what?*

To answer this question adequately, it appears to me necessary to make a detailed study of the facts, considering them in their actual historical sequence, and going back to the period before the 1949 victory in view of the prior existence of the Mao team and its rule over a considerable territory for a considerable period of time. To me it appears obvious that the nature of the Mao government in the pre-1949 days is involved.

Likewise involved is the question you point to; that is, the "manner of rule" of the national government set up in 1949. This ought to be examined within the context of the previous manner of Maoist rule. I do not doubt that a "shift" occurred—the extension of Maoist rule over all of China is an obvious instance as is the expropriation of "bureaucratic" capital. It appears to me that what would be most valuable for our movement is a detailed study of this question. I sought to suggest only a few general guidelines for this study which might in the end have to be greatly modified or junked in the light of the concrete facts.

9. It is true that our concept of the type of government that existed in the transition period has never been fully developed. There has always been a period during the leftward shift, before we could designate these states as workers states (deformed or otherwise) with workers governments at their head, that we used the term 'Workers and Peasants Government.' Even then we never clearly established what the distinctive characteristics of these governments were, nor did we identify them as the necessary 'link in the revolutionary process' that established these workers states. It seems to me that this is precisely the problem that we have to solve.

I agree with this almost wholeheartedly. I say "almost" because my memory is hazy on how we designated those governments in Eastern Europe. I wanted to check back to see if we said anything. My impression is that we did not really attempt to state the problem or solve it until the Cuban revolution occurred. I may be mistaken in this; perhaps you have already gathered the material necessary to verify this.

10. When a revolution takes place in a colonial or semicolonial country with the active participation of the masses in support of a leadership that can be either worker, peasant, or middle class can we immediately designate this as a workers and peasants government?

I would say, "No." I have in mind specifically the case of Nasserite Egypt.

11. What are the characteristics that make it a 'worker and peasant government' rather than radical bourgeois or peasant?

I would say that the chief characteristic is its direction of movement. This is indicated by its words (declared program) and its actions. The actions are decisive and we should discount the words if they prove not to coincide with the actions of the government. Some notable examples are available for study in this respect—Nasser's socialist demagogy, for instance, in contrast to his use of state power to foster a new capitalist class; and in the case of the

Cubans the opposite contrast, assurances in the first stage about maintaining property relations while their actions were to the contrary.

> 12. What would be the points of qualitative change of one to the other?

I think that we have to regard a "workers and farmers government" in the sense we have been using it as a highly transitional phenomenon. The establishment of such a government by no means leads inevitably to the establishment of a workers state as we have seen in the case of Algeria.

What is most decisive is its practice in relation to the capitalist state structure on which it rests. If a government calling itself "socialist," as in the case of Nasser's regime, simply restaffs the old state structure and intervenes in the economic structure along the lines of "statism," its direction of movement is clearly not toward establishment of a workers state. The social context is also of key importance—the involvement of the masses on a revolutionary scale is required, for this is what basically determines the direction of movement.

The relations with the imperialist powers are also fairly indicative. In the case of Algeria, for instance, the role played by imperialism in overthrowing Ben Bella and in bolstering Boumedienne was very revealing. The captains of world capitalism are exquisitely sensitive on such questions.

As to the actual points of qualitative change, we have already discussed these above in several instances, particularly Cuba.

> 13. Above all, what are the dynamics of a worker and peasant regime that make it the 'link in the revolutionary process'?

What is involved is governmental power. A party or team that gains governmental power thereby gains the possibility of smashing the old state structure and overturning capitalism.

If a revolutionary-Marxist party exists, and gains governmental power under the impulsion of a revolution, there is no question as to the subsequent dynamics. The party assures it through its program, through the cadres imbued with that program, and through the experience gained in the living class struggle that finally puts it in power. The course of the Russian revolution is a classic example. Note well, however, that the Bolsheviks held power for a period on the basis of the capitalist state structure and the capitalist economy. Time was required to carry out their program. If anything, they had to carry through these changes *prematurely*. (This had to be paid for later, as Trotsky explained, by the New Economic Policy.) Thus the Russian revolution provided the world with the first example of a "Workers and Peasants Government" in power with the task still before it of actually establishing a workers state.

> 14. Neither can I see how the Theses and discussions at the Fourth Congress of the C.I. are really applicable here. They deal essentially with the tactics used by a revolutionary party during a period of crisis when it does not yet have hegemony over the working class.

I agree that this was the main question discussed at the Fourth Congress and that the main outcome was the application of the united front policy for the purposes you indicate.

> 15. It is true that the Congress listed four different types of workers or workers and peasants governments, and listed them under these classifications in order to set their tactical orientation to each.

This was where it appeared to me that the discussion at the Fourth Congress did have a connection with the problem that faced us. I also added Trotsky's comments in the Transitional Program, which you do not mention.

Under point No. 13 above, concerning the "dynamics of a worker and peasant regime." I list the case of such a government controlled by a revolutionary-Marxist party. There is no problem for us in this instance; but the question that faced us was the appearance of similar governments in which a party comparable to the Bolshevik party either did not exist or existed as a minority. (In China it existed as a tiny minority that was brutally liquidated by the Maoists.) The Bolsheviks in their discussion excluded the possibility of such governments, controlled by petty-bourgeois parties, actually establishing workers states. They reached this conclusion largely on the basis of their experience, an experience, of course, that was determined by the development of the international class struggle and the balance of world power as it stood in their day.

We were confronted, however, by the cases of Yugoslavia, the other countries of Eastern Europe, China, North Vietnam, North Korea, and finally Cuba. We were faced with actual situations never encountered by the Bolsheviks although they had anticipated the possibility (especially Trotsky) in a very general and abstract way. (Yet to me this anticipation was highly illuminating and I once again felt what giants our predecessors were and how open they were to what life itself might bring up, and how prepared they were to make adjustments in the general forecasts advanced on the basis of previous theory and experience.)

Thus we really had no choice, if we were to live up to the norms established by our teachers, except to work out our own answer to the appearance of a decisive "link in the revolutionary process"—the link of governmental power—in which a revolutionary-Marxist party was not in control, yet which led to the establishment of a workers state (deformed or otherwise).

The problem was very important in my opinion. If we did not succeed, we were faced with the following alternatives:

Either (a) the Stalinist parties proved to be genuine revolutionary parties after all, even under Stalin. The consequence of this would be inescapable—Trotsky was wrong. This was the line of reasoning followed by Arne Swabeck in the case of China.

Or (b) petty-bourgeois forces of no matter what kind and under no matter what kind of circumstances can conceivably establish a workers state and even along the "cold road." This was the line of reasoning of those who came to the conclusion that Egypt, Syria, etc., are workers states, or, under a different label ("state capitalism," etc.) equivalents of the Soviet Union.

Or (c) the facts are inexplicable theoretically and the whole thing must be regarded as a hopeless mess. Perhaps this is the line of thinking of some of the Healyites to judge from the distaste they display in dealing with this problem.

It occurred to me that the discussions at the Fourth Congress of the Communist International, plus the intimation in Trotsky's point in the Transitional Program (under the heading "Workers and Farmers Government") about "the petty bourgeois parties, including the Stalinists," going further "than they themselves wish" along this road although it was a "highly improbable variant," offered valuable clues to a solution of the problem on the theoretical level.

It also occurred to me that if we were to decide that the "highly improbable variant" mentioned by Trotsky had actually occurred, then the events which we were compelled to explain in any case if we wished to remain true to scientific socialism might themselves offer fresh insights and an enrichment of the bare abstractions posed as excluded as a highly improbable variant by the Bolsheviks and Trotsky. I centered my efforts on the Cuban revolution which appeared to me to offer the clearest and most telling example. The results, I think, were not unfruitful.

What was especially instructive was to see the political *differentiations* that occurred in this peculiar variant and the *limitations* on the dynamics of this specific link as it actually developed in the revolutionary process. I don't want to go into that here—I have already discussed it in articles on the Cuban revolution but I mention it as a preliminary to your next question.

> 16. In the light of the Theses of the Fourth Congress how could you possibly explain a petty bourgeois leadership that emerges out of the national struggle and *as a body* with comparatively few defections goes through the transition to a workers state?

As a body. But that is not what has occurred. In the case of Cuba, which offers the clearest example, the July 26 Movement split wide open. An entire wing—the right wing—disintegrated. Some very prominent leaders during the revolutionary struggle against Batista broke from Castro and Guevara to finally end up with the gusanos. The left wing, on the other hand, moved toward socialism and finally declared the Cuban revolution to be a socialist revolution.

To be noted with special attention: This differentiation occurred *after* the July 26 Movement had come to power and while it was dealing with governmental problems on the basis of a still existing capitalist state.

> 17. I see this as a verification of the theory of permanent revolution and not of the Theses of the Fourth Congress.

I agree with the first part of your sentence. What happened in Cuba under the workers and peasants government headed by Fidel Castro certainly does verify the theory of permanent revolution.

I disagree with the second part of your sentence. In my opinion, the existence of this peculiar transitional government in Cuba offered the most striking proof of the prescience of the leaders at the Fourth Congress in foreseeing such a possibility (even though they excluded that it could actually establish a workers state). It offers just as striking proof of Trotsky's prescience in the Transitional Program when he left it open as a "highly improbable variant."

> 18. It seems to me that the solution lies in a closer examination of the national liberation struggles under the special set of circumstances that have existed from the end of World War II. They include the considerable weakening of imperialism on a world scale; the enhanced strength and prestige of the Soviet Union; the great weight and power of the colonial struggles for liberation; the reduced size, strength, and loss of confidence of the native capitalists. These were bolstered in former periods by the weight of the compradore bourgeoisie, but these sections now flee at the early stage of struggle leaving the native capitalists even weaker. Add to this the chronic crisis of the peasantry.

In this paragraph you do not deal with the specific problem but with the general context in which the problem is located. What you say about this context is true. However, I would place more stress on the general weakening of world capitalism, on the impasse of imperialism, and I would add as a primary part of the context the *default* of Stalinism. The default of Stalinism is required to explain why the liberation struggles have taken the form of *national* liberation struggles instead of *socialist* liberation struggles in such a prominent way in recent decades.

> 19. A revolutionary movement rising out of the national struggle, even under middle class leadership, sees imperialism as its main enemy and also sees a counterbalance to it—the attractive power of the Soviet Union and the other workers states. The movement feels that imperialism no longer has such overwhelming power, that it cannot be opposed or defied. There is now room for maneuver. It is no accident that there has emerged a 'third world' section, the so-called neutrals, that play both sides in an attempt to gain some advantage for themselves.

You are still dealing with the context. The paragraph appears rather abstract to me. What examples do you have in mind? Would you include Egypt? What you say would seem to hold true not only for revolutionary movements arising out of the national struggle, "even under middle-class leadership," but also for the bourgeoisie. India, for example.

> 20. The national character of the movement gives the leadership an added advantage, in that it can gain support of workers and peasants as well as the middle class and some section of the capitalists in its fight against imperialism.

Again, you are dealing with the general context of the problem and not the problem itself. What you say holds also for the bourgeoisie. It is sufficient to cite the expropriation of the oil industry in Mexico under Cárdenas in the late thirties. Cárdenas was very popular with the workers and peasants both in Mexico and throughout Latin America. A current example is the Velasco regime in Peru with its expropriations, agrarian reform, and anti-imperialist stance.

> 21. If there was a conscious revolutionary party on the scene this 'national unity'

would not exist but would separate into sharply contending wings of the class struggle. The process would then take a different road, following more closely the pattern of struggle laid out by Trotsky, where the capitalists and their reformist supporters would be progressively isolated and the workers with their peasant allies would move toward power to a workers and peasants government or directly toward a dictatorship of the proletariat.

It is hard to disagree with what you say. If this had been the situation, the revolution would have taken a quite different course in Yugoslavia, Eastern Europe, China, North Vietnam, North Korea, and Cuba. And we would have had no tough theoretical problem to bedevil us.

22. With the absence or failure of a revolutionary party to rise to the situation a petty bourgeois leadership can get the support of diverse elements and come to power on a limited, short term program meeting the new situations in its typical empirical fashion.

This is precisely the situation that requires theoretical explanation. What is a "petty bourgeois leadership" that finds itself "in power" except a "workers and farmers government" in the sense that we have been using it? If you really hold to this position, what do you object to, then, the nomenclature? But I called attention to this unfortunate nomenclature in the article mentioned above, published in the Winter 1961 *International Socialist Review*. On the other hand, if you really hold to this position, aren't you in contradiction with the substance of your paragraph (No. 1 above) stating that you do not recall such a position having been included in our resolutions and that you believe it adds something new to our theory?

I would not insist on the contradiction but it would seem that if you really hold to this position then you are logically compelled to relate it to the previous theory held by our movement; or, if there has been no previous theory, to explain the reason for its absence. I am convinced that if you were to follow through on this (leaving aside the question of nomenclature) that you would have to go back at least to the Fourth Congress of the Communist International where the question *did* come up.

23. The attitude of the imperialists is crucial. If it is hostile and adamantly opposes the leftward swing, especially nationalizations of 'its' holdings, the revolution has the option of turning to the Soviet Union for aid. Where the leadership had Stalinist origins as in Yugoslavia, China, and Vietnam this reaction would be on the order of an automatic reflex. In Cuba the turn to the Soviet Union went hand in hand with the sharpening of the struggle with Washington. If the imperialists adopt a more flexible attitude and make concessions in order to maintain some economic ties the process can be slowed down or even reversed. I think Algeria is an example of this. The lever France used was that of economic agreements, especially on the exploitation of Sahara oil.

Again, you are describing features of the context of the problem. I would call attention only to the sentence about its being an "automatic reflex" for leaders of Stalinist origins to turn to the Soviet Union. There are new elements in the context—the rebellions in East Germany, Poland, Hungary, Czechoslovakia, not to mention the Sino-Soviet rift. We should add Cuba's experience, recalling what Guevara said in Algiers about the obligation of the strong "socialist" powers to help the weaker ones and to give aid to revolutionary movements abroad. It is true in general, however, that the leaders of any upsurge will turn in the direction of the USSR, or China, or Cuba, etc., in search of material aid against imperialism. They will turn in any direction that material aid can be obtained. Nkrumah, let it be recalled, helped some of the African movements. So has Boumedienne.

24. Nationalization is a logical step for a backward country that must find the means of setting up enterprises for national survival or for trade on the world market. There is no other national source to finance them. Taking over the property of the huge imperialist monopolies is a natural starting point for national independence. The recent examples in Bolivia and Chile indicate how strong this

pressure is even on bourgeois leaders friendly to imperialism. Where the masses participate in the revolutionary process nationalization is far more sweeping, especially when Soviet aid and advice become large factors in the nationalization process. Control of foreign trade and banking become natural logical steps as measures of defense if not as positive policies to defend the gains already achieved.

We remain within the general context. How to explain the fact that not every government, whatever the pressures, responds so logically to these logically necessary steps? Only workers and peasants governments have thus far proved capable of proceeding in logical enough fashion to end up with the establishment of workers states. Why do other governments, faced with the same pressures, take the course of increasing "statism"?

I do not disagree with what you say although I would not be so categorical in stating that there is no other national source to finance enterprises or trade on the world market except through nationalization. The peasants (leaving aside the workers) remain a prime source of financing enterprises even though they may remain small landholders for a considerable time.

Also I would be a bit cautious about "Soviet aid and advice" as possible large factors in the nationalization process. As you point out earlier, Moscow is not above engaging in plunder where it is feasible; and we know for certain that most, if not all of the smaller "socialist" countries are bitterly critical of Soviet practices. It was certainly one of the elements in the Sino-Soviet rift, whatever the faults of the Chinese in this respect.

25. Thus the struggle, beginning at the level of national liberation, with the support of the masses moves on past the national level into the permanent revolution. What is essential for the process to develop into the workers state form is the maintenance of the pressures that started the revolution in the first place; a national revolutionary upsurge, a leadership responsive in some measure to the mass pressure, hostility to imperialism concretized in nationalizations, elimination of capitalist elements that oppose this process and the continued pressure of imperialism that prevents any stabilization and adaptation to a peaceful coexistence at some intermediate stage. With this also develops a socialist consciousness which has either been in the background of the movement or has been acquired in the course of the struggle.

As a general description of the revolutionary process as a whole in the colonial and semicolonial spheres, what you say is correct. However, you leave out (although you come to it in your next paragraph) the role of governmental power in this process. For the purposes of our discussion, this is the decisive item.

26. Does a government that carries out these measures have to be a workers and peasants government?

I am not sure what you have in mind. Are you thinking of Egypt or some of the other African and Middle Eastern countries? What would be implied is the possibility of other kinds of governments establishing workers states. Even more, that some of these countries are already workers states.

27. Could it not be carried out by a petty bourgeois government or even a national coalition of anti-imperialist forces at least in the early stages?

This goes even further despite the saving phrase "at least in the early stages."

28. The experiences of the twenties and thirties indicated that when the middle class was caught between class pressures the majority invariably gravitated toward capitalism. With the relationships changed in the post World War II period it is more possible for sections of the middle class, when under the pressure of the mass movement, to gravitate towards the working class. This has apparently happened in a few special cases.

In the context of the two previous questions, I am not sure what you have in mind. On the face of it, you seem to be merely describing how much more favorable this aspect of the class struggle is today than in the twenties and thirties. Again on the face of it, you seem to have left out completely the problem at hand—the nature of the governmental power that can establish a workers state in the colonial and semicolonial areas in the absence of a revolutionary-Marxist party.

29. It is clear that the negative features persist in this development. While they follow the main line of permanent revolution the transition is not thorough nor complete. They result in deformed or incompleted workers states and remain on the national level. Where they go beyond the national level it is solely as a measure of national defense. While the leaderships have opposed or eliminated threats from the right they equally oppose tendencies from the left that try to move the struggle to the international level.

This is too general, for we are still left with the problem of tracing developments on the level of governmental power so that these can be properly fitted into the overall context. Because these sentences are so general they lead to speculation as to what countries you have in mind.

These are my reactions to your letter, Bob. I am sorry I could not go into some of the points of special interest in detail. On the other hand, if you would take just one country and check out in detail what happened on the single level of the changes in governmental power, this would advance the discussion considerably. There are various countries on which little has been done in this field as you know. At the convention I suggested that work of this kind on the Chinese revolution might prove fruitful, but I think the same holds true of several other countries where it may be easier to obtain the necessary materials.

Fraternally yours,
Joseph Hansen

SECTION TWO: BACKGROUND MATERIALS ON THE 'WORKERS AND FARMERS GOVERNMENT'

1. The workers government—Excerpts from the 'Theses on Tactics' and discussion at the Fourth World Congress of the Comintern

Following are extracts from the documents of the Fourth World Congress of the Communist International held in late 1922. The first item, "The Workers Government" is point eleven of the "Theses on Tactics" adopted by the congress. It appears here in a new translation from the French by Michael Baumann. Second is an excerpt from the Fourth Congress discussion on the "Theses on Tactics." This debate took place from November 9 till November 12, 1922. The third item is excerpts from the discussion on "The Capitalist Offensive." These excerpts are taken from abridged transcripts of the debates at the Fourth Congress on November 11, 16, and 17, 1922.

XI. The workers government

The call for a workers government (eventually a government of the peasants as well) should be raised everywhere as a *general propaganda slogan*. But as a slogan of present-day political activity, the call for a workers government takes on its greatest importance in countries where the situation of bourgeois society is particularly unstable, where the relationship of forces between the workers parties and the bourgeoisie puts on the agenda, as a political necessity, the solution to the question of a workers government.

In these countries, the slogan of a "workers government" is an inevitable consequence of the entire united-front tactic.

The parties of the Second International are seeking to "save" the day in these countries by calling for and forming coalitions between the bourgeoisie and the Social Democrats. In their most recent attempts to do this, certain parties of the Second International (in Germany, for example) refused to participate openly in a coalition government of this sort in order to bring it into being in a disguised fashion. This was no more than a maneuver intended to calm the masses who were protesting against such coalitions; it was no more than a sophisticated swindle of the working masses. To the coalition between the bourgeoisie and the Social Democrats, whether it be open or concealed, the Communists counterpose the united front of all workers and the political and economic coalition of all workers parties against bourgeois power, in order to overthrow the latter once and for all. In the common struggle of all these workers against the bourgeoisie, the entire state apparatus must fall into the hands of the workers government, and in this way the position of the working class will be strengthened.

The most elementary program of a workers government must consist in arming the proletariat, disarming the counterrevolutionary bourgeois organizations, installing supervision over production, insuring that the main burden of taxation falls on the rich, and smashing the resistance of the bourgeois counterrevolution.

A government of this sort is only possible if it emerges from the struggle of the masses themselves, if it is based on working-class organizations that are suited for combat and formed by the broadest layers of the oppressed working masses. A workers government resulting from a parliamentary combination may also provide an opportunity for strengthening the revolutionary workers movement. But it goes without saying that the emergence of a genuine workers government and the continued existence of a government carrying out a revolutionary policy must lead to a fierce struggle and, eventually, to a civil war with the bourgeoisie. The proletariat's mere attempt to form a workers government will immediately encounter the most violent resistance on the part of the bourgeoisie. The slogan of a workers government is therefore capable of giving a focus to and setting off revolutionary struggles.

In certain circumstances, Communists should declare that they are prepared to form a government with workers parties and organizations that are non-Communist. But they can take such an action only when guarantees are given that these workers governments will really carry out a struggle against the bourgeoisie in the sense indicated above. In this case, the normal conditions for Communists' participation in such a government would be the following:

(1) Participation in a workers government can take place only with the approval of the Communist International;

(2) The Communist members of a workers government remain under the strictest control of their party;

(3) The Communist members of a workers government remain in direct contact with the revolutionary organizations of the masses;

(4) The Communist Party has the absolute right to maintain its public identity and retains complete independence of agitation.

Despite its great advantages, the slogan of a workers government also has its dangers, just as any united-front tactic has. As a precaution against these dangers, the Communist parties should not lose sight of the fact that, although every bourgeois government is at the same time a capitalist government, it is not true that every workers government is actually proletarian, that is, a revolutionary instrument of proletarian power.

The Communist International should anticipate the following possibilities:

(1) A liberal workers government. There is already a government of this sort in Australia; there may also be one before very long in England.

(2) A Social-Democratic workers government (Germany).

(3) A workers and peasants government. This is possible in the Balkans, Czechoslovakia, etc.

(4) A workers government in which Communists participate.

(5) A genuine proletarian workers government which, in its purest form, can only be represented by a Communist Party.

The first two types of workers governments are not revolutionary workers governments, but rather governments that camouflage a coalition between the bourgeoisie and the counterrevolutionary leaders of the working class. In a critical period, these "Workers Governments" are tolerated by a weakened bourgeoisie in order to deceive the proletariat as to the real class character of the state or, with the assistance of corrupt working-class leaders, to derail the revolutionary offensive of the proletariat and gain time. Communists must not participate in such governments. To the contrary, they must relentlessly expose to the masses the real character of these phony "workers governments." In the period of the decline of capitalism, a period in which the principal task consists in winning a majority of the proletariat over to the revolution, these governments can objectively contribute to accelerating the process of the decomposition of the bourgeois regime.

Communists are prepared to march with workers—Social Democrats, Christians, non-party, syndicalist, etc.—who have not yet recognized the need for the dictatorship of the proletariat. Under certain circumstances and with certain guarantees, the Communists are equally prepared to support a non-Communist workers government. But the Communists must at all costs explain to the working class that its liberation can only be assured by the dictatorship of the proletariat.

The other two types of workers governments are types that the Communists can participate in, although they still do not represent the dictatorship of the proletariat; they do not represent a necessary form of transition toward the dictatorship, but they can serve as a point of departure for attaining this dictatorship. The full dictatorship of the proletariat can only be accomplished by a workers government composed of Communists.

FROM THE DISCUSSION ON THE THESES BY THE COMINTERN DELEGATES NOVEMBER 9–12, 1922. (ABRIDGED REPORT PUBLISHED IN LONDON.):

ZINOVIEV: (reporting for the Executive Committee of the Communist International) . . . The watchword of the Labour Government has not yet been fully clarified. The tactics of the united front are almost universally applicable. It would be hard to find a country where the working class has attained notable proportion but where the tactics of the united front have not yet been inaugurated. They are equally applicable in America, in Bulgaria, in Italy, and in Germany. By no means can the same thing be said of the watchword of the Labour Government. This latter is far less universally applicable, and its significance is comparatively restricted. It can only be adopted in those countries where the relationships of power render its adoption opportune, where the problem of power, the problem of government, both on the parliamentary and on the extraparliamentary field, has come to the front. Of course, even today in the United States good propaganda work can be done with the slogan of the Labour Government. We can explain to the workers "If you want to free yourselves, you must take power into your own hands." But we cannot say, in view of the present relationships of power in the United States, that the watchword of the Labour Government is applicable to an existing fight between two parties, as it has been in Czechoslovakia, as it will be perhaps in Germany, and as it was and may be again in Italy.

The watchword of the Labour Government then is not a general watchword like the tactics of the united front. The watchword "Labour Government" is a particular concrete application of the tactics of the united front under certain specific conditions. It is quite easy to make mistakes in this matter. I think we have to beware of the danger that results from an attempt to regard the stage of Labour Government as a universally necessary one. Insofar as it is safe to prophesy in such matters, I myself incline to the view that a Labour Government will only come into existence occasionally, in one country or another, where peculiar circumstances prevail. I think its occurrence will be exceptional. Besides, it is quite a mistake to suppose that the formation of a Labour Government will inaugurate a quasi-peaceful period, and that thereby we shall be saved from the burden of the struggle. The working class must be made clearly to understand that a Labour Government can only be a transitional stage. We must say in plain terms that the Labour Government will not do away with the need for fighting, will not obviate the necessity for civil war. But as long as we recognize the dangers of this watchword, we need not hesitate to employ it. . . .

ERNEST MEYER: (Germany) . . . The most difficult question which we had to solve in connection with the United Front tactics—(and which we have probably not yet solved)—is the question of the Workers Government. We must differentiate between social democratic governments in Germany—in Saxony, Thuringia and formerly also in Gotha—governments which we had to support but which have nothing in common with what we understand by Workers Government. If we desire that the International should support the idea of the Workers Government, and if we wish that this watchword should be adopted by the brother parties that are working approximately under similar conditions to ours, this does not mean that we expect them to aim at the establishment of social democratic governments and to participate in them, but merely that they should struggle for Workers Governments, thus making our struggle easier. The chief difference between a workers and a social-democratic government is—that the former, without bearing the label of a socialist policy, is really putting socialist-communist policy into practice. Thus, the Workers Government will not be based on parliamentary action alone, it will have to be based on the support of the wide masses, and its policy will be fundamentally different from that of the social democratic governments such as those existing in some of the countries of Germany.

Today Comrade Zinoviev made this distinction between a workers government and proletarian dictatorship. This was never made quite clear before when this discussion was discussed. We find the following statement by Comrade Zinoviev on page 123 of the report on the session of the Enlarged Executive:—

> The workers government is the same as the dictatorship of the proletariat. It is a pseudonym for Soviet Government. (Hear, hear.) It is more suitable for the ordinary working man, and we will therefore use it.

According to our conception this is wrong. The workers government is not the dictatorship of the proletariat (quite so, from the German Delegation), it is only a watchword which we bring forward, in order to win over the workers and to convince them that the proletarian class must form a United Front in its struggle against the bourgeoisie. Should this watchword be followed or adopted by the majority of the working class, and should the latter take up the struggle for this aim in good earnest, it will soon become evident that the attempt to bring about this workers government (at least in most countries with a big proletarian population) will lead either directly to the dictatorship of the proletariat or to a prolonged phase of very acute class struggles, namely, to civil war in all its forms.

In that respect we consider the slogan of the workers government as necessary and useful to winning over the masses. It will lead to a sharper class conflict from which the Proletarian Dictatorship will finally arise. . . .

RADEK: . . . With regard to the demand for a Workers Government. A Workers Government is not the Proletarian Dictatorship, that is clear; it is one of the possible transitory [transitional] stages to the proletarian dictatorship. The possibility of such a transitory stage is due to the fact that the working masses in the West are not so amorphous politically as in the East. They are members of parties and they stick to their parties. In the East, in Russia, it was easier to bring them into the fold of Communism after the outbreak of the revolutionary storm. In your countries it is much more difficult. The German, Norwegian and Czechoslovakian workers will more readily declare against coalition with the bourgeoisie, preferring a coalition of labour parties which would guarantee the eight-hour day and an extra crust of bread, etc. A Workers Party usually arises in this manner, either through preliminary struggles or on the basis of a parliamentary combination, and it would be folly to turn aside the opportunities of such a situation in stubborn doctrinaire fashion.

Now the question arises—shall we recline upon this soft cushion and take a good rest, or shall we rather lead the masses into the fight on the basis of their own illusions for the realization of the program of a Workers Government? If we conceive the Workers Government as a soft cushion, we are ourselves politically beaten. We would then take our place beside the social-democrats as a new type of trickster. On the other hand, if we keep alive the consciousness of the masses that a Workers Government is an empty shell unless it has workers behind it forging their weapons and forming their factory councils to compel it to hold on to the right track and make no compromise to the Right, making that government a starting point for the struggle for the proletarian dictatorship, such a Workers Government will eventually make room for a Soviet government and not become a soft cushion, but rather a lever for the conquest of power by revolutionary means. I believe one of the comrades has said, "The Workers Government is not a historic necessity but a historical possibility." This is, to my mind, a correct formula. It would be absolutely wrong to assert that the development of man from the ape to a People's Commissar must necessarily pass through the phase of a Workers Government. (Laughter.) Such a variant in history is possible, and in the first place it is possible in a number of countries having a strong proletarian and peasant movement, or where the working class overwhelmingly outnumber the bourgeoisie, as is the case in England. A parliamentary labour victory in England is quite possible. It will not take place in the present elections, but it is possible in the future, and then the question will arise: What is the Labour government? Is it no more than a new edition of the bourgeois-liberal government, or can we compel it to be something more? I believe Austen Chamberlain was right in saying, "If a Labour government comes into power in England, it will begin with a Clynes' administration and end in a government of the Left Wing, because the latter can solve the unemployed problem."

Thus, Comrades, I believe that the Executive on the whole has taken the right attitude in this question, when on the one hand it warns against the proposition of either Soviet government or nothing, and, on the other hand, against the illusion which makes the Workers Government a sort of parachute. . . .

DURET: (France) . . . There is another side to the tactics of the United Front which, regardless of all my efforts, still passes my understanding. I am speaking of the question of the Workers Government.

Comrade Thalheimer has used five or six pages to explain to me what is meant by a Workers Government. But I am hard-headed. I failed to understand. Comrade Radek has made an attempt at explaining the same subject in more ample fashion, but still I fail to understand. It seems that I will have to give it up as a bad job. . . .

BORDIGA: (Italy) . . . As to the watchword of the Workers Government, if we can be assured—as was the case of the enlarged Executive of last June—that it means nothing else but the "revolutionary mobilization of the working class for the overthrow of bourgeois domination," we find that in certain cases it might replace that of the dictatorship of the proletariat. In any case, we would not be opposed to it, unless it be used as an opportunistic attempt to veil the real nature of our program. If this watchword of the labour government were to give to the working masses the impression that the essential problem of the relations between the proletarian class and the state—on which we based the program and the organization of the International—can be solved by any other means than by armed struggle for power in the form of proletarian dictatorship, then we will reject this tactical method because it jeopardizes a fundamental condition of the preparation of the proletariat and of the party for the revolutionary tasks in order to achieve the doubtful success of immediate popularity. . . .

GRAZIADEI: (Italy) . . . Let us pass to the conception of the Workers Government. It is quite possible that in a country where a large section of the working class is still imbued with bourgeois or semi-bourgeois democratic ideas, a Workers Government may find support, for some time, in the trade unions, on the one hand, to which we must attach increasing political importance, and on a parliamentary form on the other. We cannot reject the Workers Government because it may for a short time take a parliamentary form. This would be a great mistake. In Russia, after the March revolution, the Communists attempted to increase the political power of the Soviets in which they were still a minority, but they did not abandon Parliament when a purely social-democratic government was in power. In Germany, after the fall of the Empire, we found Parliament and the Soviets side by side.

Naturally the Communists must always teach the workers that a real workers government can only be formed as a result of armed revolt against the bourgeoisie, and that this government must be under the control of its class organizations. They must continually teach the workers that if the dictatorship of the proletariat is not attained very soon, the workers government will not be able to resist the assaults of the bourgeoisie. . . .

MARKLEVSKY: (Poland) . . . I would like to speak a few words on the slogan of the Workers Government. I believe there has been too much philosophical speculation on the matter. ("Very true," from the German benches.) The criticism of this slogan is directed on three lines—the Workers Government is either a Scheidemann government or a coalition government of the Communists with the social traitors. It finds support either in parliament or in the factory councils. It is either the expression of the dictatorship of the proletariat, or it is not. I believe that philosophical speculation is out of place—for we have practical historical experience. What did the Bolsheviks do in 1917 before they conquered power? They demanded "All Power to the Soviets." What did this mean at that time? It meant giving power to the Mensheviks and the Social Revolutionaries who were in the majority in the Soviets. It meant at that time a Workers Government in which social traitors participated, and which was directed against the dictatorship of the proletariat. But this slogan was a good weapon of agitation in the hands of the Bolsheviks.

It may be that a great revolutionary movement will start at a time when we will not yet have conquered the majority of the proletariat. But when it comes the ferment will enable us to win over the majority of the proletariat much more rapidly than we can now, and the slogan we will then put forward in all probability will be essentially the slogans which the Executive, in one form or another, attempted to formulate. The government we will then demand will be essentially the Workers Government, but based on the masses. If the Executive has failed to formulate a solution for this question it is because we have mixed our terms and have attempted to give our slogans a definite form when they are really dependent upon revolutionary circumstances. . . .

DOMBSKY: (Poland) . . . As regards the workers government, I was in the same boat as my friend Comrade Duret, I could not understand the meaning of workers government in our tactics. At last I have heard a clear definition of this government. Comrade Radek has solaced me in private conversation that such a government is not contemplated for Poland. (Comrade Radek: "I never said that.") Oh, then Poland will also have to bear the punishment of this sort of government. It is thus an international problem. Comrade Radek says that the workers government is not a necessity but a possibility, and it were folly to reject such possibilities. The question is whether if we inscribe all the possibilities on our banner we try to accelerate the realization of these possibilities. I believe that it is quite possible that at the eleventh hour a so-called workers government should come which would not be a proletarian dictatorship. But I believe when such a government comes, it will be the resultant of various forces such as our struggle for the proletarian dictatorship, the struggle of the social-democrats against it and so forth. Is it proper to build our plans on such an assumption? I think not, because I believe that we should insist on our struggle for the proletarian dictatorship.

This does not mean to say that we ought not to make any partial demands.

KOLAROV: (Balkan Communist Federation) . . . The problem of the workers government does not arise in the agricultural Balkan countries, and therefore I will not dwell on it. . . .

ZINOVIEV: (summarizing) Comrades, you will allow me to discuss in some detail the question of Workers Government. It is not yet quite clear to me whether there are serious differences of opinion with regard to this question, whether this question has been completely ventilated, or whether a good deal of our differences were caused by variations in terminology. In the course of the Congress, and during the working out of the resolution on tactical questions, with which we shall deal after the question of the Russian Revolution, this will become clear. As far as I am concerned, the question has nothing to do with the word "pseudonym" which has been quoted here. I am quite willing under these circumstances, to give up the word. But the main thing is the significance. I think, comrades, that the question will be made clear if I express myself as follows: It is clear to us that every bourgeois government is a capitalist government. It is hard to imagine a bourgeois government—the mule of the bourgeois class—which is not at the same time a capitalist government. But I fear that one cannot reverse that saying. Every working class government is not a proletarian government; not every workers government is a socialist government.

This contrast is radical. It reveals the fact that the bourgeoisie have their outposts within our class, but that workers have not their outposts within the capitalist class. It is impossible for us to have our outposts in the camp of the bourgeoisie.

Every bourgeois government is a capitalist government, and even many workers governments can be bourgeois governments according to their social composition. I think that the main point is, there are workers governments and workers governments. I believe that one can imagine four kinds of workers governments, and even then we will not have exhausted the possibilities. You can have a workers government which, according to its composition, would be a liberal workers government, for example, the Australian Labour Government. Several of our Australian comrades say that the term workers government is incorrect because in Australia we have had such workers governments of a bourgeois nature. These were really workers governments, but their composition was of a purely liberal character. They were bourgeois workers governments, if one may so term them.

Let us take another example: The general elections are taking place in England. It is not probable, but one may as well accept in theory, as a possibility, that a workers government will be elected which will be similar to the Australian Labour Government, and will be of a liberal composition. Thus a liberal workers government in England can, under certain circumstances, constitute the starting point of revolutionizing the situation. That could well happen. But by itself, it is nothing more than a liberal workers government. We, the Communists, now vote in England for the Labour Party. That is the same as voting for a liberal workers government. The English Communists are compelled, by the existing situation, to vote for a liberal workers government. These are absolutely the right tactics. Why? Because this objective would be a step forward; because a liberal government in England would disturb the equilibrium and would extend the bankruptcy of capitalism. We have seen in Russia during the Kerensky regime how the position of capitalism was smashed, despite the fact that the liberals were the agents of capitalism. Plekhanov, in the period from February to October, 1917, called the Mensheviks semi-Bolsheviks. We say that this was an exaggeration. They were not semi-Bolsheviks, but just quarter-Bolsheviks. We said this because we were at war with them, and because we saw their treachery to the proletariat. Objectively, Plekhanov was right. Objectively, the Menshevik government was best adapted to make a hash of capitalism by making its position impossible. Our party, which was then fighting the Mensheviks, would not and could not see this. The parties stood arrayed for conflict. Under such conditions, we can only see that they are traitors to the working class. They are not opponents of the bourgeoisie, but when, for a period, they hold the weapons of the bourgeoisie in their hands, they make certain steps which are objectively against the bourgeois state. Therefore, in England, we support the liberal workers government and the Labour Party. The English bourgeoisie are right when they say that the workers government will start with Clynes and finish in the hands of the Left Wing.

That is the first type of a possible workers government.

The second type is that of a Socialist government. One can imagine that the United Social Democratic Party forms a purely Socialist government. That would also be a workers government, a Socialist government, with the word—Socialist—of course in quotation marks. One can easily imagine a situation where we would give such a government certain conditional credit, a certain conditional support. One can imagine a Socialist government as being a first step in the revolutionizing of the situation.

A third type is the so-called coalition government; that is, a government in which Social-Democrats, Trade Union leaders, and even perhaps Communists, take part. One can imagine such a possibility. Such a government is not yet the dictatorship of the proletariat, but it is perhaps a starting point for the dictatorship. When all goes right, we can kick one social-democrat after another out of the government until the power is in the hands of the Communists. This is a historical possibility.

Fourthly, we have a workers government which is really a workers government—that is, a Communist workers government, which is the true workers government. I believe that this fourth possibility is a pseudonym for dictatorship of the proletariat, that it is truly a workers government in the true sense of the word. This by no means exhausts the question. There can be a fifth or sixth type, and they can all be excellent starting points for a broader revolutionizing of the situation.

But, in order to construct a workers government in the revolutionary sense, one must overthrow the bourgeoisie; and that is the most important. We must not forget that we have here to distinguish between two things: (1) Our methods of agitation; how we can best speak to the workers, how we can enable them best to understand the position. For that purpose, I believe the slogan of "Workers Government" is best adapted. (2) How will events develop historically, in what concrete forms will the revolution manifest itself?

We must look at the question from all sides. It is nevertheless difficult to make any prediction. If we now look at the slogan of the workers government from this new standpoint, as a concrete road to the realization of the proletarian revolution, we may doubt whether the world revolution must necessarily pass through the stage of the workers government. Our friend Radek said yesterday that the workers government is a possible intermediary step to the dictatorship of the proletariat. I agree, it is a possibility, or more exactly an exceptional possibility. This does not mean that the slogan of the workers government is not good. It is a good instrument of agitation where the relation of forces makes it possible. But if we put this question: is the workers government a necessary step towards the revolution? I must answer that this is not a question that we can solve here. It is a way, but the least probable of all. In countries with a highly developed bourgeois class, the proletariat can conquer power by force alone, through civil war. In such a case an intermediary step is not to be thought of. It might take place, but it is useless to argue here about it. All that is necessary is that we see clearly all the possible ways towards the revolution. The workers government may be nothing more than a liberal Labour government, as it might be in England and in Australia. Such a workers government can also be useful to the working class. The agitation for a workers government is wise, we may gain many advantages therefrom. But in no case must we forget our revolutionary prospects. I have here a beautiful article by the Czechoslovak minister, Benisch. I will read you a passage.

The "Tschas," organ of Minister Benisch, writes, on September 18: "The Communist Party is building the United Front of the Workers on a slogan of a fight against unemployment.

"We cannot deny that the Communists are clever. They know how to present to the workers the same thing under different forms. For instance, some time ago, the Communists began a campaign for the formation of Soviets. When they saw that this campaign was unsuccessful, they stopped their agitation, but it resumed a year and a half later under the mask of United Front committees. The United Front of the proletariat might become a tremendous force if based on progressive ideas, but the ideas of Moscow are not progressive."

This bourgeois is right, I believe. We Communists who deal with the masses intellectually enslaved by the bourgeoisie, must take all efforts to enlighten our class. I have said that a workers government might be in reality a bourgeois government. It is our duty to enlighten in all ways the more receptive sections of the working class. But the contents of our declaration must always remain the same.

Another thing, comrades, Soviet government does not always mean dictatorship of the proletariat. Far from it. A Soviet government existed for eight months in Russia parallel with the Kerensky government, but this was not a dictatorship of the proletariat. Nevertheless, we defended the slogan of the Soviet government, and only gave it up for a very short time.

This is why I believe that we can adopt the policy of the workers government with a peaceful heart, under the only condition that we do not forget what it really amounts to. Woe to us if we ever allow the suggestion to creep up in our propaganda that the workers government is a necessary step, to be achieved peacefully as a period of semi-organic construction which may take the place of civil war, etc. If such views exist among us, we must combat them ruthlessly; we must educate the working class by way of telling them—"Yes, dear friends, to establish a workers government, the bourgeoisie must be first overthrown and defeated."

The International must adopt the right tactics, but there are no tactics by means of which we could outwit the bourgeoisie and glide smoothly into the realm of the workers government. The important thing is that we overthrow the bourgeoisie, after which various forms of the workers government may be established. . . .

FROM THE DISCUSSION ON 'THE CAPITALIST OFFENSIVE.' NOVEMBER 11, 16 AND 17, 1922.

RADEK: (reporting) . . . In the concluding portion of my speech, Comrades, I propose to deal briefly with the watchwords of the struggle.

Agreed, that the starting points of our activities must be the demand for higher wages, the demand for the retention of the eight-hour day, and the demand for the development of the industrial union council movement. But these demands do not suffice. Workers who belong to no political party at all can and do demand the daily wage of one thousand marks, whilst five hundred marks will not procure them the necessaries of life. But they see that to increase their wages in paper money provides no issue from their trouble. To begin with, such watchwords may suffice; but the longer the struggle lasts, the more essential does it become to proclaim political watchwords, the watchwords of social organization. When the time is ripe for the voicing of such demands, it is time to move from the defensive to the offensive. We must put forward in these circumstances the demand for the control of production and make clear to the workers that this is the only way out of economic chaos.

Now I come to a question which plays a great part in our resistance to the capitalist offensive. I refer to the question of the Labour Government. The important point for us in this connection is, rather than classification, to propound the question: What are the masses of the workers, not merely the Communists, thinking of when they speak of Labour Governments? I confine myself to countries in which these ideas have already been considered: Britain, Germany and Czechoslovakia. In England, think of the Labour Party. Communism there is not yet a mass power. In the countries where capitalism is decaying, this idea is intimately associated with that of the United Front. Just as the workers say that the meaning of the United Front is that the Communists and the Social-Democrats must make common cause in the factory when there is a strike, so for the masses of the workers the idea of a Labour Government has a similar significance. The workers are thinking of a government of all the working class parties. What does that mean for the masses practically and politically? The political decision of the question will depend upon the fact whether the social-democracy does or does not go to its doom with the bourgeoisie. Should it do so, then the Labour Government can only take the form of the dictatorship of the Communist proletariat. We cannot decide for the Social Democrats what their policy should be. What we have to decide is this. When we lead the masses in the struggle against the capitalist offensive, are we ready to fight on behalf of such a labour coalition government? Are we or are we not ready to bring about the conditions essential to its realization?

That is a question which for the masses would only be confused by theoretical calculations. In my opinion, when we are concerned with the struggle for the United Front, we ought to say bluntly that, if the social democratic workers will force their leaders to break with the bourgeoisie, then we are ready to participate in a labour government, so long as that government is an instrument of the class struggle. I mean, if it is ready to fight beside us shoulder to shoulder.

When we are thinking of the struggle against the capitalist offensive, what we have in mind is not a parliamentary combination, but a platform for the mobilization of the masses, an arena for the struggle.

As far as we are concerned with the broad front of the proletarian struggle for freedom, the watchword of the labour government is necessary to supply us with a directive; it is a watchword that whets the edge of our political weapons. The moment when the workers find themselves simultaneously engaged in the fight for the Labour Government and in the fight for the control of production, will be the moment when our fundamental offensive will begin, the moment when we shall cease to content ourselves with trying to defend what we have, and shall advance to the attack on new positions. Our offensive will begin as soon as the masses of the workers are ready to fight for these two watchwords.

RAVENSTEIN: (Holland) . . . Comrade Trotsky drew attention to the danger of reformist and pacifist illusions in the Western Parties. Well, in the light of the experiences of last year, there can be no two opinions on that score. But he went on to say that the political background for such illusions would probably be extremely favourable for some time to come. This view he based on the assumption that the political developments of the Western countries will quite easily lead to a bloc, and consequently to a government of petty-bourgeois pacifist elements, a bloc of the left, so to speak, which would lay claim to the support of the Labour parties. In such a contingency there would be considerable danger of such a bloc gaining support from Communists, or at least an inclination to such support, but I am of the opinion that the time has gone by for these blocs of the left, and they will never come back again.

Democracy is being shattered by the "right." This is the dominating factor of present-day politics in all the old bourgeois countries, like England, France, Belgium and Holland. . . .

This development of events knocks out the bottom of the labour parties and even of the reformist and pacifist bourgeois groups....

In conclusion, I wish to point out that it is an altogether mistaken idea to expect either Henderson and Clynes in England or Longuet and Blum in France, to be able to form a government relying upon the bourgeois reformist elements. The Hendersons and the Clynes, Longuets, Vanderveldes and Troelstras could only serve their highest purpose as ministers in an imperialist United Front. But the imperialist United Front could certainly not be brought within the strict definition of the terms of Workers Government.

I, therefore, come to the conclusion that the proletarian United Front is the great tactical line of guidance in all capitalist states, where the proletariat has not yet been victorious without any distinction of their respective history, culture and tradition. On the other hand, the workers government can be considered only for special circumstances that may arise in Central Europe and perhaps in other countries. For these countries it has its greatest value. But only under the method of the United Front of the entire proletariat can the Communist International fight and win throughout the world.

STERN: (Austria) . . . The slogan of the workers government is a counter move against the slogan of a coalition government. The United Front is no longer a measure of defense, it has already become a weapon of offense.

RADEK: (in reply) . . . So long as we represent the weaker section of the working class movement we will have to deal with the social democrats, although we know that the leaders of the social democracy are conscious enemies of the revolution. But it may happen that the social democrats should betray the bourgeoisie instead of the working class. . . . Should the pressure of the masses force the social democrats to give up their coalition policy, we will be ready to fight our common enemy, the bourgeoisie, together with them. We must not only maintain our ideological purity; we must take part in the daily struggles of the workers. . . .

How does the British Communist Party apply its United Front tactics? . . . The Executive has shown in its manifesto to the workers that the entire policy of the Labour Party is nothing but a continuous betrayal of working class interests. But the Executive also said to the workers: "If the Labour Party is victorious and forms a government, it will betray you in the end and will show to the workers that its aim is the perpetuation of capitalism. Then the workers will either desert it, or the Labour Party will be compelled to fight owing to the pressure of the workers, and in that case we shall back it. We issued a definite watchword: 'Vote for it, but prepare to struggle against it.'"

2. The call for a workers government in France
By Leon Trotsky

The following article by Leon Trotsky was written in November 1922, in conjunction with the adoption of the resolution, "A Militant Program of Action for the French Communist Party," by the Fourth World Congress of the Communist International. The first known publication of this article was in *Bulletin Communiste no. 7*, dated February 15, 1923. It also appears in *Le mouvement communiste en France* by Pierre Broué (Editions de Minuit, Paris. 1967, p. 214). "A Workers Government in France" was translated from the French by Joseph Hansen for inclusion in this collection.

"Workers government" is an algebraic formula, that is, a formula in which numerical values have not been set. Hence its advantages and also its drawbacks.

Its advantages lie in its reaching out to workers who have not yet grasped the idea of a dictatorship of the proletariat nor comprehended the necessity of a guiding party.

Its drawbacks, deriving from its algebraic nature, lie in the fact that a purely parliamentary meaning can be given to it, which for France would be the least realistic practically and the most dangerous imaginable ideologically.

Léon Blum could say: "A workers government is acceptable to us. As soon as the working class gains a parliamentary majority, we will be ready to form a workers government."

Interpreted in that way, it is quite evident that a workers government will never be established in France, since in practice the politics of Léon Blum, Jouhaux and Company consists of making blocs with the bourgeoisie while "waiting" for this workers parliamentary majority, blocs that in turn exclude the possibility of forming a workers majority inasmuch as they disrupt and demoralize the working class.

Thus the slogan calling for a workers government in France is not a slogan for parliamentary combinations—it is a slogan for mobilizing the masses of workers to break completely from parliamentary combinations with the bourgeoisie, to close ranks against the bourgeoisie and advance the idea of their own government against all the bourgeois governmental combinations. So that this algebraic formula is in essence profoundly revolutionary.

But, it might be said, precisely because it is revolutionary and not parliamentary won't it be rejected by the political dissidents and the workers who follow them? That is possible. But if we prove capable of skillfully utilizing our slogan in agitation, the dissident workers who may reject it at first will not reject it later on.

We can say to them: "You are for democracy and for a parliamentary majority. We will not keep you from getting a workers majority in Parliament. To the contrary, we will help you in every way. But to achieve that, the whole working class must be mobilized. The workers have to see that their interests are involved; a slogan must be provided capable of uniting and strengthening them. This slogan can be none other than a workers government, in opposition to all the bourgeois combinations and coalitions. So that to create a workers majority in Parliament, a powerful movement must be set going in the working class and in the peasant masses under the slogan of a *workers government*." That is how, from the angle of agitation, the question must be posed to the dissidents and to the reformist workers, etc. This way of posing the question is correct, politically and pedagogically.

But is a workers government realizable in France in any form except that of a Communist dictatorship, and, if so, in what form?

In certain political conjunctures, it is perfectly realizable; and it is, in fact, an inevitable stage in the development of the revolution.

Indeed, if in a violent political crisis a powerful mobilization of the workers in the country leads to elections resulting in a majority for the dissidents and the Communists, including the intermediate and sympathizing groups, and the mood of the working masses does not permit the dissidents to make a bloc with the bourgeoisie against us, it will be possible, under these conditions, to form a coalition workers government constituting a necessary transition toward the revolutionary dictatorship of the proletariat.

It is quite possible, it is even likely, that such a mobilization, developing under the slogan of a workers government, will occur too speedily to be reflected in a parliamentary majority, either because there is no time for new elections, or because the bourgeois government will try to ward off this threat by resorting to Mussolini's methods. In putting up resistance to the fascist attack, the reformist party of the working class could be drawn by the Communist party onto the road of forming a workers government by *extraparliamentary* means. Under this hypothesis, the revolutionary situation would be even clearer than under the former.

In the latter case would we agree to form a coalition government with the dissidents? We would—if they still had a considerable following in the working class that could force them to break away from the bourgeoisie. Would this assure us against any betrayal by our allies in the government? Not at all. While working with them in the government to carry out the initial revolutionary steps, we would have to watch them just as vigilantly as we would watch an enemy; we would have to ceaselessly consolidate our political positions and *our organization*, preserve our freedom of criticism with regard to our allies and weaken them by ceaselessly presenting new proposals that would break up the combination by driving more and more of the right-wing elements to split away.

As for the working-class party of the dissidents, under the conditions indicated above it would be absorbed little by little into the Communist ranks.

These are some of the possibilities of actually realizing the idea of a workers government in the course of the development of a revolution. But at the present time, it is precisely because of its algebraic character that this formula is politically important to us. Right now, it provides a general perspective for the whole struggle for immediate demands, provides a general perspective for the struggle not only for the Communist workers, but for the broad masses that have not yet come over to Communism, by linking them, by uniting them with the Communists through the unifying effect of a common task. This formula is the capstone of the policy of the United Front. In every strike that is defeated because of government and police repression, we will say: "This wouldn't happen if representatives of the workers were in power instead of the bourgeoisie." Every time there is a legislative measure directed against the workers, we will say: "This wouldn't have happened if all the workers were united against the bourgeoisie, if they had created their workers government."

The idea is simple, clear, convincing. Its power lies in the fact that it is in line with historic developments. It is precisely because of this that it entails the greatest revolutionary consequences.

L. Trotsky
NOVEMBER 30, 1922

3. From 'An Explanation in a Circle of Friends'
By Leon Trotsky

The following excerpt is the concluding section of "An Explanation in a Circle of Friends (On the Elements of Dual Power in the USSR)" which first appeared in the November–December 1931 issue of the Russian-language *Biulleten Oppozitsii* (number 25–26). The translation by Tim Burnett was prepared for *Writings of Leon Trotsky (1930–31)*, where the complete article will be found.

Here Trotsky expresses sharp opposition to the use of the slogan "Workers and Peasants Government," counterposing the demand for a "Workers Government" to it. The slogan "Workers and Peasants Government" was used by the Stalinized Comintern to express a two-stage theory of revolution. It was also a companion of the Stalinist practice of supporting supposedly two-class "workers and peasant parties" (like the Kuomintang in China), which attributed an independent political role to the peasantry.

Trotsky later revised his opinion of the slogan and decided that the slogan calling for a "workers and peasants government" was correct provided it was filled with a revolutionary content and not counterposed to the dictatorship of the proletariat. His later views appear in the section of "The Death Agony of Capitalism and the Tasks of the Fourth International" entitled "Workers' and Farmers' Government".

How do you view the slogan 'Workers and Peasants Government?'

In general, it is a negative one, and especially for Germany. Even in Russia where the agrarian question played a decisive role and where we had a revolutionary peasant movement, we did not put forward this slogan, even in 1917. We spoke about a government of the proletariat and the village poor, that is, the semiproletarians following the proletariat. Through this the class character of the government was fully defined. True, subsequently we called the Soviet government worker and peasant. But by this time, the dictatorship of the proletariat was already a fact, the Communist Party was in power, and consequently the name Workers and Peasants Government could not give rise to any ambiguity or grounds for alarm. But let's turn to Germany. To put forward here the slogan of workers and peasants government as it were, putting the proletariat and the peasantry on the same footing, is completely incongruous. Where, in Germany, is there a revolutionary peasant movement? In politics it is impossible to work with imaginary or hypothetical quantities. When we speak of a workers government then we can explain to a farm laborer that the question is of a government that will protect him from exploiters even if they are peasants. When we speak of a worker and peasant government then we confuse the farm laborer, the agricultural worker, who in Germany is a thousand times more important to us than the abstract "peasant" or the "middle peasant" who is hostile to us. We can only get to the peasant poor in Germany through the agricultural workers. We can only neutralize the intermediary layers of peasants by rallying the proletariat under the slogan of a workers government.

Are the references to Lenin in support of the slogan a 'Workers and Peasants Government' correct?
Totally incorrect. The slogan itself was put forward as far as I remember between the Fourth and Fifth Congresses of the Comintern as a weapon in the struggle against "Trotskyism." The formation of the famous Krestintern [Peasant International] took place under this slogan. The secretary of the Krestintern, Teodorovich, formulated a new Marxist slogan, "The liberation of the peasants must be the work of the peasants themselves." To this epigonic ideology the slogan of a "workers and peasants government" fully corresponds; it has nothing in common with Leninism.

SEPTEMBER 2, 1931
L.T.

4. From 'The Death Agony of Capitalism and the Tasks of the Fourth International'

Following is the section entitled "Workers' and Farmers' Government" from *The Death Agony of Capitalism and the Tasks of the Fourth International* (The Transitional Program). The Transitional Program was adopted by the founding congress of the Fourth International in 1938, and remains a central programmatic document of world Trotskyism. This excerpt is reprinted from *The Transitional Program for Socialist Revolution* (Pathfinder Press, New York, first edition, 1973, third edition, 2014), pp. 172-76.)

Workers' and farmers' government
This formula, "workers' and farmers' government," first appeared in the agitation of the Bolsheviks in 1917 and was definitely accepted after the October Revolution. In the final instance it represented nothing more than the popular designation for the already established dictatorship of the proletariat. The significance of this designation comes mainly from the fact that it underscored the idea of an *alliance between the proletariat and the peasantry* upon which the Soviet power rests.

When the Comintern of the epigones tried to revive the formula buried by history of the "democratic dictatorship of the proletariat and peasantry," it gave to the formula of the "workers' and peasants' government" a completely different, purely "democratic," i.e., bourgeois content *counterposing* it to the dictatorship of the proletariat. The Bolshevik-Leninists resolutely rejected the slogan of the "workers' and peasants' government" in the bourgeois-democratic version. They affirmed then and affirm now that when the party of the proletariat refuses to step beyond bourgeois-democratic limits, its alliance with the peasantry is simply turned into a support for capital, as was the case with the Mensheviks and the Social Revolutionaries in 1917, with the Chinese Communist Party in 1925–27, and as is now the case with the People's Front in Spain, France, and other countries.

From April to September 1917, the Bolsheviks demanded that the S.R.'s and Mensheviks break with the liberal bourgeoisie and take power into their own hands. Under this provision the Bolshevik Party promised the Mensheviks and the S.R.'s, as the petty-bourgeois representatives of the workers and peasants, its revolutionary aid against the bourgeoisie; categorically refusing, however, either to enter into the government of the Mensheviks and S.R.'s or to carry political responsibility for it. If the Mensheviks and the S.R.'s had actually broken with the Cadets (liberals) and with foreign imperialism, then the "workers' and peasants' government" created by them could only have hastened and facilitated the establishment of the dictatorship of the proletariat. But it was exactly because of this that the leadership of petty bourgeois democracy resisted with all possible strength the establishment of its own government. The experience of Russia demonstrated, and the experience of Spain and France once again confirms, that even under very favorable conditions the parties of petty bourgeois democracy (S.R.'s, Social Democrats, Stalinists, Anarchists) are incapable of creating a government of workers and peasants, that is, a government independent of the bourgeoisie.

Nevertheless, the demand of the Bolsheviks, addressed to the Mensheviks and the S.R.'s: "Break with the bourgeoisie, take the power into your own hands!" had for the masses tremendous educational significance. The obstinate unwillingness of the Mensheviks and S.R.'s to take power, so dramatically exposed during the July Days, definitely doomed them before mass opinion and prepared the victory of the Bolsheviks.

The central task of the Fourth International consists in freeing the proletariat from the old leadership, whose conservatism is in complete contradiction to the catastrophic eruptions of disintegrating capitalism and represents the chief obstacle to historical progress. The chief accusation which the Fourth International advances against the traditional organizations of the proletariat is the fact that they do not wish to tear themselves away from the political semi-corpse of the bourgeoisie. Under these conditions the demand, systematically addressed to the old leadership: "Break with the Bourgeoisie, take the power!" is an extremely important weapon for exposing the treacherous character of the parties and organizations of the Second, Third, and Amsterdam Internationals. The slogan, "workers' and farmers' government," is thus acceptable to us only in the sense that it had in 1917 with the Bolsheviks, i.e., as an anti-bourgeois and anti-capitalist slogan, but in no case in that "democratic" sense which later the epigones gave it, transforming it from a bridge to socialist revolution into the chief barrier upon its path.

Of all parties and organizations which base themselves on the workers and peasants and speak in their name we demand that they break politically from the bourgeoisie and enter upon the road of struggle for the workers' and farmers' government. On this road we promise them full support against capitalist reaction. At the same time we indefatigably develop agitation around those transitional demands which should in our opinion form the program of the "workers' and farmers' government."

Is the creation of such a government by the traditional workers' organizations possible? Past experience shows, as has already been stated, that this is to say the least highly improbable. However, one cannot categorically deny in advance the theoretical possibility that, under the influence of completely exceptional circumstances (war, defeat, financial crash, mass revolutionary pressure, etc.) the petty bourgeois parties including the Stalinists may go further than they themselves wish along the road to a break with the bourgeoisie. In any case one thing is not to be doubted: even if this highly improbable variant somewhere at some time becomes a reality and the "workers' and farmers' government" in the above-mentioned sense is established in fact, it would represent merely a short episode on the road to the actual dictatorship of the proletariat.

However, there is no need to indulge in guesswork. The agitation around the slogan of a workers'-farmers' government preserves under all conditions a tremendous educational value. And not accidentally. This generalized slogan proceeds entirely along the line of the political development of our epoch (the bankruptcy and decomposition of the old bourgeois parties, the downfall of democracy, the growth of fascism, the accelerated drive of the workers toward more active and aggressive politics). Each of the transitional demands should, therefore, lead to one and the same political conclusion: the workers need to break with all traditional parties of the bourgeoisie in order, jointly with the farmers, to establish their own power.

It is impossible in advance to foresee what will be the concrete stages of the revolutionary mobilization of the masses. The sections of the Fourth International should critically orient themselves at each new stage and advance such slogans as will aid the striving of the workers for independent politics, deepen the class character of these politics, destroy reformist and pacifist illusions, strengthen the connection of the vanguard with the masses, and prepare the revolutionary conquest of power.

5. On the slogan of 'workers and farmers government'
By Michel Pablo

The following article by Michel Pablo appeared in French in the June–July 1946 issue of *Quatrième Internationale*, published by the secretariat of the Fourth International. The following translation is reprinted from the February 1947 issue of *Fourth International*, predecessor to the *International Socialist Review*. Pablo was a veteran Greek Trotskyist who became the central leader of European Trotskyism and secretary of the Fourth International for nearly a decade after World War Two. Beginning in 1949, he put forward theories and organizational concepts that led to a de facto split in the International in 1953. He broke with the Trotskyist movement shortly after its reunification in 1963.

The formula, "workers' and farmers' government" first appeared in 1917 in the policy of the Bolsheviks.

In this instance it assumed two aspects. 1) As a general propaganda slogan it represented a popular designation for the dictatorship of the proletariat "underscoring the idea of an alliance between the proletariat and poor peasantry upon which the Soviet power rests," as our Transitional Program states. 2) As a slogan of current policy, it was concretized, between April–September 1917, by the Bolsheviks, then still a minority in the Soviets, as the demand addressed to the Mensheviks and Socialist-Revolutionaries to "break the coalition, and take the power into their own hands." This had an enormous educational value for the masses.

The theme of this article is this second aspect of the question. The slogan of the "workers' and farmers' government," sanctioned by the Bolshevik experience of 1917, was definitively endorsed by the Communist International after the October insurrection.

In particular the Fourth Congress of the Communist International in its *Resolution on Tactics* revived the slogan in both these aspects, but it especially insisted upon its importance as a slogan of current policy. We know that subsequently the Communist International of the epigones, whenever it attempted to revive the formula of the "democratic dictatorship of the proletariat and peasantry" in the colonial countries, and after 1934 through its Popular Front policy the world over, as our Transitional Program correctly states, "gave to the formula of 'workers' and peasants' government' a completely different, purely 'democratic,' i.e. bourgeois content." Our movement has always rejected this interpretation and whenever it has used this formula, as for example during the first period of the Spanish Revolution and in France between 1934–1936, it has done so in the manner of the Bolshevik experience of 1917 and of the Communist International up to 1923.

To arrive at a correct understanding of the formula, "workers' and farmers' government," as a slogan of current policy, it is therefore necessary to study this experience concretely.

The Bolshevik experience

The formula of the "workers' and farmers' government" as a slogan of current policy is meaningful only under certain given conditions characterized by a relationship of forces between the parties claiming to represent the working class and the bourgeoisie which "places on the order of the day as a political necessity the solution of the question of the workers' government." (Resolution on tactics of the Fourth Congress of the C.I. The Transitional Program justifies the use of this slogan by analogous arguments.) Under these conditions the revolutionary party which is still a minority in the working class addresses the demand to the majority working class parties to "break the coalition, take the power," and carry out a genuine working class policy.

That is what the Bolsheviks did between April–September 1917. Let us briefly review the characteristic features and events of this period. On March 14, 1917 the first provisional government presided over by Prince Lvov was formed, as a result of an agreement with the Soviets of Workers' and Soldiers' Deputies dominated by the Mensheviks and Socialist-Revolutionaries. This government continued up to the crisis of May 3–5, 1917. On May 18, after the resignation of Milyukov, the first coalition government was formed, presided over again by Prince Lvov with the participation of the "Socialist" delegates from the Petrograd Soviets.

This government continued until the July Days of 1917 when it gave way to the second coalition government presided over by Kerensky. During this entire period from March until the July Days a regime of dual power existed in Russia: On the one side the political government of the bourgeoisie and on the other side the Councils of workers, peasants and soldiers. Lenin considered this period from March 12 to July 17 as the period of expansion of the effective power and democracy of the Soviets, conditions which guaranteed the peaceful development of the Revolution by means of ideological struggle of the workers' parties within the Soviets.

The Bolsheviks, for their part, represented on the national plane during this period a small minority in the Soviets. (At the First All-Russian Congress of the Soviets on June 16, dominated by the Menshevik delegates, the Bolsheviks represented barely 13 per cent. Moreover, at the First All-Russian Congress of peasant delegates held at Petrograd from May 17 to June 11 the Bolshevik fraction was insignificant.)

Under these conditions the Bolsheviks went through this entire democratic period of the revolution with two essential slogans: "All power to the Soviets" and "Down with the capitalist Ministers."

In the given relationship of forces within the Soviets this meant in practice that the power would pass into the hands of the Mensheviks and the Socialist-Revolutionaries who held the majority there.

Consequently the formula "All power to the Soviets, Down with the capitalist Ministers" meant in practice the demand "for a Menshevik-Socialist-Revolutionary Government."

Lenin expressly admitted this when for example during the Kornilov *coup d'etat* he proposed that his party offer a conditional compromise to Kerensky by calling for "the return to our pre–July Days slogan of all power to the Soviets, of a government of Mensheviks and Socialist-Revolutionaries responsible to the Soviets."

The Bolshevik demand addressed to the "Socialists" during this period had a revolutionary meaning precisely because it was not a question of the formation of a parliamentary government, but of a government based upon the Soviets and controlled by the Soviets.

Moreover, during this same period the Soviets, effectively assuming power were a) the sole armed force of the people against which the bourgeois government was absolutely impotent, and b) the democratic form *par excellence* of the free expression of the majority which could be won over by ideological struggle alone. Lenin found these conditions sufficed to reject any idea of a violent transfer of power to the proletarians and semi-proletarians, recommending on the contrary ideological struggle within the Soviets.

Replying to the criticisms of the Menshevik press, which accused the Bolsheviks of inciting the workers not only against the government but also against the Soviets, he wrote: "In Russia we have now enough liberty to be in a position to make the will of the majority prevail through the composition of the Soviets of workers' and soldiers' representatives. Consequently, if the proletarian party desires seriously (and not in the Blanquist manner) to take power, we ought to struggle to gain influence in the Soviets. All this has been said, repeated, and explained again and again in *Pravda* and only stupid or malicious people cannot understand it." Further on, in the same article: "We have a right for which we are going to fight: We will fight to acquire influence and the majority in the Soviets. We repeat again: We will declare ourselves in favor of transferring power into the hands of proletarians and semi-proletarians only when the Soviet of representatives of workers and soldiers adopts our policies and is disposed to take this power into its hands."

We have another very clear example of the anti-capitalist, revolutionary interpretation of the slogan, "workers' and farmers' government," concretized in the formula "Menshevik-Socialist-Revolutionary government," on the occasion of Kornilov's *coup d'etat*.

As we have already pointed out, Lenin regarded the slogan "All Power to the Soviets" as perfectly in order for an entire period "of a possible peaceful development of the Revolution in April, May, June, up to the days of July 12–22, that is to say, up to the moment when actual power passed into the hands of the military dictatorship (of Kerensky)." After Kerensky unleashed the terror against the working class and against the Bolsheviks in particular, that is to say, after the freeing of the government from effective control by the Soviets, their decline into impotence, and the stifling of democracy within them, Lenin considered: "that this slogan is no longer correct because it does not take into account the accomplishment of the passage of power (into the hands of a military dictatorship) and of the real and total betrayal of the Revolution by the Mensheviks and Socialist-Revolutionaries." Lenin thereupon called upon the workers' vanguard to declare for "a decisive struggle," to abandon every "constitutional or democratic illusion," every illusion regarding a "peaceful" development.

However, in the first days of September came the revolt of Kornilov, his march from the front toward the capital to overthrow Kerensky and proclaim himself dictator.

Kerensky and his "socialist" Ministers, submitting to the pressure of the masses, determined to defend the endangered Revolution with arms in hand, saw themselves forced to struggle against the reactionary general.

Just at this crucial moment the opportunists in the ranks of the Bolshevik Party raise their voices to express, if only indirectly, a kind of confidence in the provisional government to "defend it (in common) against the Cossacks." They propose a bloc with the "Socialists" to "support" the government.

An important lesson

The position Lenin took on this question contains a lesson of tremendous educational value for all the revolutionary parties concerning the Leninist application of the united front tactic and of the "workers' and farmers' government" slogan which, under certain political circumstances is an inevitable consequence of the latter.

Lenin was for the immediate expulsion from the Party of the defenders of the bloc with the "Socialists." (*Rumors of Conspiracy*, August 31, 1917.)

In his letter to the Central Committee of the Bolshevik Party dated September 12, 1917 Lenin thus defined his position toward the Kerensky government:

> And *even now* we must not support Kerensky's government. That would be unprincipled. It will be asked: What, not even fight Kornilov? Of course, fight him! But that is not the same thing; there is a dividing line, that line is being overstepped by certain Bolsheviks, who allow themselves to become "compromisers" and to be *carried away* by the flood of events.
>
> We will fight and are fighting Kornilov, *just as Kerensky's troops are*. But we do not support Kerensky; *on the contrary*, we expose his weakness. That is the difference. It is a rather subtle difference, but an extremely important one, and must not be forgotten.
>
> What change, then, is necessitated in our tactics by the Kornilov revolt?
>
> We must change the *form* of our struggle against Kerensky. While not relaxing our hostility towards him one iota, while not withdrawing a single word we uttered

against him, while not renouncing the aim of overthrowing Kerensky, we say: We must *reckon* with the present state of affairs; we shall not overthrow Kerensky just now; we shall adopt a *different* method of fighting him, namely, we shall point out to the people (who are fighting Kornilov) the *weakness and vacillation* of Kerensky. That was done *before* too. But now it has become *the main thing*. That is the change.

The change, furthermore, consists in this, that *the main thing* now is to intensify our agitation in favor of what might be called "partial demands" to be addressed to Kerensky, namely: arrest Milyukov; arm the Petrograd workers; summon the Kronstadt, Viborg and Helsingfors troops to Petrograd; disperse the State Duma; arrest Rodzyanko; legalize the transfer of the landlords' estates to the peasants; introduce workers' control over bread and over the factories, etc. These demands must be addressed not only *to* Kerensky, and *not so much* to Kerensky as to the workers, soldiers and peasants who have been *carried away* by the struggle against Kornilov.

Draw them still further; encourage them to beat up the generals and officers who are in favor of supporting Kornilov; urge *them* to demand the immediate transfer of land to the peasants; suggest *to them* the necessity of arresting Rodzyanko and Milyukov, of dispersing the State Duma, of shutting down *Rech* and the other bourgeois papers, and instituting proceedings against them. The "Left" Socialist-Revolutionaries particularly must be pushed in this direction.

As to the talk of defence of the country, of a united front of revolutionary democracy, of supporting the Provisional Government, and so forth, we must oppose it ruthlessly as mere *talk*.

Returning to this question of "compromise" with Kerensky against Kornilov in his article "On Compromises" of September 14, Lenin thus set forth the conditions:

> The compromise would amount to this: that the Bolsheviks, without making any claim to participate in the government (which is impossible for the internationalists until a dictatorship of the proletariat and the poor peasantry is actually realized), would refrain from demanding the immediate transfer of power to the proletariat and poor peasants and from employing revolutionary methods of fighting for this demand. A condition, one that is self-evident and not new to the Socialist-Revolutionaries and the Mensheviks, would be complete freedom of propaganda and the convocation of the Constituent Assembly without further delay, or even at an earlier date than that appointed.
>
> The Mensheviks and the Socialist-Revolutionaries, as the governmental *bloc*, would agree (assuming that the compromise is reached) to form a government responsible solely and exclusively to the Soviets, and also to the transfer of the entire power to the Soviets in the localities. This would constitute the "new" condition. No other condition would, I think, be advanced by the Bolsheviks, confident that, with full freedom of propaganda and with the immediate realization of a new democracy in the composition of the Soviets (new elections) and in their functioning, the peaceful progress of the revolution and a *peaceful solution* of the party strife within the Soviets would be guaranteed.

Among other things, what is interesting in Lenin's position are the two conditions for the compromise he lays down for the "united front" proposed to Kerensky: a) full freedom of propaganda in the Soviets; b) returning effective power to the local Soviets. This is very important. Once again Lenin refuses to *support* a "Menshevik-Socialist-Revolutionary government," assumes no political responsibility for its actions, but promises only to resume the road of peaceful progress of the Revolution within the Soviets reconstituted with full powers and democratic organization, and consequently to tolerate the government of the "Socialists" as long as it is the emanation of the freely expressed will of the Soviet majority.

In conclusion, to understand the real meaning of the formula, "workers' and farmers' government" given by the Bolshevik experience of 1917 as a slogan of current policy, it is necessary to take into account the following conditions:

a) The demand of the Bolsheviks addressed to the Mensheviks and Socialist-Revolutionaries was to be placed in the framework of the existence of a united front organized by all the workers' parties, the Soviets, having effective power and complete internal democracy. The Government was to be based on the Soviets and controlled by them. It would therefore be a Government of the type of the Commune, within the framework of a genuine democratic workers' republic.

b) Even under these conditions the Bolsheviks would not support such a government, would not assume any political responsibility for its actions, but they would tolerate it only in so far as it was the emanation of the freely expressed will of the majority of the Soviets.

c) The Bolsheviks did not in the least restrict their propaganda in the Soviets to have their point of view adopted by the Soviets and consequently by the Government of the Soviets.

It is necessary to keep constantly in mind all of these conditions to understand the true transitional, anti-capitalist and revolutionary significance of the formula, "workers' and farmers' government" employed between April and September 1917 by the Bolsheviks.

The Communist International revived this formula in the same sense. The aforecited resolution on tactics adopted by the Fourth Congress of the C.I. is perfectly clear on this point. After having emphasized that this formula as a slogan of *current policy* acquires an importance when the relationship of forces between the workers' parties and the bourgeoisie places on the order of the day the question of a workers' government, the resolution specifies that this slogan "is an inevitable consequence of the whole tactic of the united front." But what united front, of what extent, on what program? The resolution gives a clear answer to all these questions.

What is involved is not a united front of a temporary and restricted character to attain certain limited objectives, on a program of economic demands, such as a trade union united front. It is a question of a much broader plan of action.

"To the *open* or *masked* bourgeois and Social-Democratic coalition," specifies the resolution, "the communists oppose the united front of all the workers, and *the political and economic* coalition of all the workers' parties against the bourgeois power for the definitive overthrow of the latter."

The communists themselves define in their propaganda what the program of such a government ought to be:

> The most elementary program of a workers' government must consist in arming the proletariat, in disarming the counter-revolutionary bourgeois organizations, in establishing control over production, in imposing upon the rich the main weight of taxation and breaking the resistance of the counter-revolutionary bourgeoisie.

Our Transitional Program explains this matter in the same sense when it says:

> Of all parties and organizations which base themselves on the workers and peasants and speak in their name we demand that they break politically from the bourgeoisie and enter upon the road of struggle for the workers' and farmers' government. On this road we promise them full support against capitalist reaction. At the same time, we indefatigably develop agitation around those transitional demands which should in our opinion form the program of the workers' and farmers' government.

The more recent examples of the Spanish and French experiences further illustrate the practical use of this slogan and its meaning.

The Spanish experience

In April 1931 King Alfonso left Spain and the Republic was proclaimed.

The Spanish revolution began. Its first steps in 1931, with the governments of Zamora-Maura and Lerroux, in which the "socialist" ministers predominated, recall the provisional governments of March to July 1917 in Russia.

There was, however, an essential difference between the two situations: the action of the masses in Russia was channelled from the first in the extra-parliamentary organization of the Soviets, while in Spain there were no Soviets in 1931. Because of this fact the bourgeois parliament, the Cortes, acquired considerable importance and the formula of the "workers' and peasants' government" was concretely translated in the Spanish situation in a different manner than in Russia.

The radicalization of the Spanish masses was manifested in 1931 in the forward thrust of the Socialist Party which quickly became the leading parliamentary party.

Nevertheless the Socialists refused to take over the entire power by themselves on the pretext that they did not have an absolute majority in the Cortes.

In his letters addressed to the leaders of the Spanish Left Opposition, Trotsky outlined the following tactic for this period: During the formation of the first coalition government of Zamora-Maura and before the June elections he recommended the slogan "Down with Zamora-Maura" which was the equivalent of the Bolshevik slogan "Down with the capitalist ministers."

Proceeding from the proposition that the Spanish workers' vanguard was interested in pushing the socialists to take complete power and force them to break the coalition, he reasoned along these lines:

> The slogan "Down with Zamora-Maura" is perfectly apropos. It is only necessary to clarify one question: the communists do not agitate in favor of minister Lerroux, nor assume the slightest responsibility for the socialist ministry; but, on every occasion, they deal their most decisive blows against the most determined and consistent class enemy, thereby weakening the conciliators themselves and opening the road for the proletariat. The communists say to the socialist workers: "Unlike us, you have confidence in your socialist leaders; therefore make them at least take power. In *that* we will honestly help you. After that, let us see what happens and who is right. (Letter on the Spanish Revolution, June 24, 1931.)

Returning to this question after the socialist victory in the June elections, he wrote:

Let us consider a bit how the Spanish workers *en masse* may view things: their leaders, the socialists, have the power. This increases the demands and the tenacity of the workers. Every striker figures that not only does he not have to fear the government but on the contrary must hope for its aid. The communists ought to take advantage of the preoccupations of the workers precisely in the following way: "Make demands upon the Government, it is your leaders who are part of it." The socialists will claim in their replies to the workers' delegations that they do not yet have the majority. The answer is clear: With a truly democratic electoral system and the breaking of the coalition with the bourgeoisie the majority is assured. But that is what the socialists do not want.

It is clear from these citations, what is involved is not supporting or propagandizing for a parliamentary socialist government applying its program, but above all addressing the socialist workers and promising them revolutionary aid against bourgeois reaction in case they force their leaders to break effectively with the coalition and take power.

But can power be won through the parliamentary road? This hypothesis is not theoretically excluded in certain exceptional conditions. What is important is not *how* a "workers" government is formed, but the *kind of action* (purely parliamentary or revolutionary) which it undertakes afterwards and the *program* it tries to carry out.

The aforementioned resolution of the Communist International envisages the possibility of a "workers" government arising from a parliamentary combination which can "provide the occasion for reanimating the revolutionary workers' movement."

Nevertheless, to leave no illusion about the significance of such a government if perchance it should be formed, the same resolution adds: "It goes without saying that the birth of a genuine workers' government and the maintenance of a government carrying out a revolutionary policy must lead to the bitterest struggle and eventually to civil war against the bourgeoisie."

Trotsky who did not advise directly counterposing Soviets to the Cortes, democratically elected "on the basis of genuinely universal and equal suffrage for all men and women of 18 years of age," nevertheless adds in the very same letter:

> All the above arguments will remain suspended in midair if we limit ourselves exclusively to democratic slogans and their parliamentary refraction. There can be no question of such a limitation. The communists participate in all strikes, all protests and demonstrations, always raising up new sections of the population. The communists participate in the struggle with the masses and in the front ranks of the masses and the base of these struggles, the communists put forward the slogan of Soviets and, on the first occasion, form the Soviets as *organizations of the proletarian united front*.

Thus the experience with the formula of the "workers' and farmers' government" as a slogan of current policy in the given conditions of the Spanish situation, despite its peculiarities, leads to the same conclusions as the Bolshevik experience: The revolutionary party in the minority demands of the majority workers' parties (either in the Soviets or in the Parliament) that they break the coalition, that they take power.

At the same time the revolutionary party conducts untiring propaganda around a program of transitional demands which in its opinion should constitute the program of the "workers' government," supported and controlled by the organized masses.

The French experience

Let us now turn to the French experience. Between February 1934 and June 1936 France passed through a profound political and social crisis proceeding from the upsurge on February 6, 1934 of the reactionary and fascist forces which imposed upon the country the "preventive Bonapartist" government of Doumergue to the powerful wave of proletarian revolt of the days of May–June 1936. Trotsky devoted a series of articles and brochures to the most profound examination of this situation, a study which provides us, among other things, with rich information concerning the meaning and use of the formula of "workers' and farmers' government" as a slogan of current policy.

After the reactionary and fascist *coup d'etat* of February 6, the Socialists and Communists, under pressure of the masses, urged a "united front against fascism," to include the Radical-Socialists. From 1936 on this was the notorious "Popular Front." But in 1934 this united front had no program against fascism. Trotsky concluded that the most important consequence of this united front, embracing at this period the whole of the public political activity of the two parties, must be "the struggle for power." (*Whither France?*) "The aim of the united front can be only a government of the united front, i.e. a Socialist-Communist government, a Blum-Cachin ministry."

This must be said openly. If the united front takes itself seriously, it cannot divest itself of the slogan of conquest of power. By what means? Trotsky replies: "By every means which leads to that end."

"The struggle for power," he writes, making his thought more precise, "means the utilization of all the possibilities provided by the semi-parliamentary Bonapartist regime to overthrow this regime by a revolutionary push, to replace the bourgeois state by a workers' state."

This argumentation has particular pertinence for those people who envisage the creation of a "workers' government" solely under conditions of a parliamentary victory of the workers' parties, which assure them the majority.

Trotsky explains that it is the offensive campaign for the conquest of power and its revolutionary program, which will unleash the strength and enthusiasm of the masses and tear them away from their parliamentary and democratic conservatism. Trotsky writes:

> The struggle for power must begin with the fundamental idea that if opposition to further aggravation of the situation of the masses under capitalism is still possible, no real improvement of their situation is conceivable without a revolutionary invasion of the right of capitalist property. The political campaign of the united front must base itself upon a well elaborated *transitional program*, i.e. on a system of measures which

with a workers' and farmers' government can assure the transition from capitalism to socialism.

Moreover, he specifies the nature of the action the united front ought to employ to achieve its aim, the taking of power:

> A concentrated campaign in the working class press pounding steadily on the same key; real socialist speeches from the tribune of parliament, not by tame deputies but by leaders of the people; the utilization of every electoral campaign for revolutionary purposes; repeated meetings to which the masses come not merely to hear the speakers but to get the slogans and directives of the hour; the creation and strengthening of the workers' militia; well organized demonstrations driving the reactionary bands from the streets; protest strikes; an open campaign for the unification and enlargement of the trade union ranks under the banner of resolute class struggle; stubborn, carefully calculated activity to win the army over to the cause of the people; broader strikes; more powerful demonstrations; the general strike of toilers of town and country; a general offensive against the Bonapartist government for the workers' and farmers' power.

The French experience with the formula of "workers' and farmers' government" in 1934 is especially interesting because it shows us among other things how little the revolutionary spirit is impeded by arguments which invoke the impossibility of conquering power through the parliamentary road, to justify passivity under the conditions of a twofold drive of the menacing reaction and the radicalized masses.

The present experience
With the end of the war, we witnessed a powerful impulsion of the masses, at least throughout Europe, toward the parties which spoke for the working class, the Communist and Socialist. This was the manifestation of the first stage of the radicalization of the masses. In many European countries these parties have even on the parliamentary plane the majority.

Their real power is actually much greater than the parliamentary refraction, necessarily falsified by the operation of a voting system which practically excludes youth, often women, as well as the omnipotence of the political machinery of the bourgeoisie, of its administration, press and all its means of manufacturing public opinion.

On the other hand, in this first stage of the radicalization of the masses, the revolutionary party, represented by the sections of the Fourth International, is still weak and cannot intervene as an independent factor.

All of these conditions make the formula "workers' and farmers' government"—as a slogan of current policy taken in its anti-capitalist and revolutionary sense—more timely than ever.

It is the central slogan of this period, the dorsal spine of all the transitional demands. As our Transitional Program correctly says "each of our transitional demands ought to lead to one and the same political conclusion: the workers ought to break with the traditional parties of the bourgeoisie to establish, together with the peasants, their own power."

The concrete application by our young sections of our Transitional Program, elaborated in 1938 before the war, but which did not really become *actual* until now, has not occurred without deviations. The press of our European sections in particular has more than once given an incorrect interpretation to the central transitional slogan *par excellence* of the "workers' and farmers' government," either in a sectarian fashion, or more often, in an opportunist sense.

The interpretation of this formula is sectarian when it is used solely as a slogan of general propaganda, i.e. as a popular designation for the dictatorship of the proletariat in such circumstances that, presented in this way, it arouses virtually no response amongst the masses. This error has been committed for example by our Greek comrades who summoned the masses to struggle for the "workers' and farmers' government," in the sense of the dictatorship of the proletariat, at the very moment when these masses were grouped in their overwhelming majority throughout the country around the Greek Communist Party and its "front" organization, the EAM.

To promote the political experience of these masses who had undeniable revolutionary aspirations meant that in Greece the formula, "workers' and farmers' government," should have been concretized in the slogan: "The EAM (purged of its bourgeois elements) to power."

The tactical task in Greece consisted in teaching the proletarian and semi-proletarian masses (poor peasants, petty-bourgeois masses) who followed the EAM, and wanted the "Laocracy," that is, a regime of the people, that they should break with the so-called bourgeois democrats (who were more insignificant than anywhere else thanks to the acuteness of the class struggle in Greece) and compel the Communist Party and the few other formations speaking for the working class and the poor peasantry grouped around it, to take the power.

At the same time, our comrades should have conducted untiring propaganda around a precise program of transitional demands (which all have an excellent field of application in Greece) and which, in our opinion, should constitute the program of this government. The Greek comrades neglected to pass from general propaganda for the "workers' and farmers' government" to its adaptation to the given situation, and it required the energetic intervention of the International to have them change their tactic.

Another sectarian deviation from this formula consists in presenting it as designed to "unmask" the treacherous nature of the parties and organizations of the Second and Third Internationals.

We are sure that the final result of this demand constantly addressed to the old "communist" and "socialist" leadership: "Break with the bourgeoisie, take power," given their almost organic incapacity to separate themselves from the political semi-corpse of the bourgeoisie, will be to reveal their treacherous character to the masses. But, in this case as with the entire tactic of the united front, this demand is not a simple maneuver on our part, but a sincere appeal to the workers to force their parties to break with the bourgeoisie, and *along this road, even if this rupture is partially realized, we will support them with all our might against every attack of bourgeois reaction*. That is the kind of language we should speak to the workers.

Let us now come to the opportunist interpretation of the formula "workers' and farmers' government" which is more frequent and more dangerous, because it can divert the whole of our politics onto a centrist basis.

We have seen this deviation develop within our French section. The last Congress of the P.C.I. has already provided the occasion for conducting a preliminary discussion on this question and to bring to light the two different interpretations given the slogan "C.P.-S.P.-C.G.T. government" used by our French section.

There are comrades who conceive of this formula as purely *parliamentary and democratic*, a minimum demand which has no connection with the "workers' and farmers' government." The reason given is that this formula can be employed, it seems, only in its general propaganda sense, that is to say "as a popular designation for the dictatorship of the proletariat." That, it seems, sums up the Bolshevik experience with this slogan. On the other hand the campaign for the "workers' and farmers' government" cannot be launched without "posing by this very fact the candidacy of the revolutionary party for this government." One reads in the same article of this comrade: "The Workers' and Farmers' Government is on the order of the day when the revolutionary party, carrying with it an important fraction of the proletariat, prepares for the dictatorship." Proceeding from these considerations, they reject this formula for the present period as "equivocal," "inopportune," and "dangerous."

But in that case, what is meant when the slogan, "C.P.-S.P.-C.G.T. government" is launched?

That concerns, we learn to our great astonishment, a tactical question, namely to formulate "the necessity of a 'C.P.-S.P.-C.G.T. government' in the event of an electoral victory of the workers' parties, and only in the event where a parliamentary majority has been obtained!" This parliamentary government will apply *its program* and although it is in reality "a bourgeois government called to administer the interests of the bourgeoisie," our party will say to the "communist" and "socialist" workers: "We are ready to march with you . . . *to support* this government that you recognize as your own; we are ready to defend it with you, against its enemies and false bourgeois friends, to allow it to realize its program, which up to now is your program!" And this unimaginable confusion is called the application of the united front tactic with the workers' parties on a minimum program and on the parliamentary plane! (Our author, in effect, conceives that this use of the slogan of a "C.P.-S.P.-C.G.T. government" flows from a united front policy with the communists and socialists, on the basis of their program, and on the parliamentary field.)

Poor united front tactic, poor Bolshevik experience, poor resolution of the Fourth Congress of the C.I., poor Transitional Program!

Everything here is entangled in inextricable confusion.

Conclusions

This article will have achieved its purpose if it succeeds in demonstrating:

a) That the formula of "workers' and farmers' government" has two aspects: one as a slogan of general propaganda, serving as a popular designation for the dictatorship of the proletariat. The other as a slogan of current policy under the following given conditions: such a relationship of forces between the workers' parties and the bourgeoisie that the solution of the workers' government becomes a political necessity.

b) That this second aspect is the one that especially interests the revolutionary party in a situation characterized by the attachment of the masses to the traditional workers' parties, while it itself remains as yet weak.

c) Under these conditions, the utilization of the formula "workers' and farmers' government" must be put forward concretely as a transitional, anti-capitalist and revolutionary demand addressed to the old leadership: "Break with the bourgeoisie, take power into your own hands."

d) "Break with the bourgeoisie" necessarily means to apply not the program of these parties, which is precisely the program of the coalition, but an effective working class, anti-capitalist and revolutionary program.

It can sometimes happen that the program of the "workers" government can be in large part the program defended by the Communist Party, or the Socialist Party, or by their united front. This can occur only in the exceptional circumstances that these parties advance a really revolutionary program, at least on paper. In this case we will try to compel their leadership to bring this program before the masses and to engage in struggle for its realization.

Such was the case, for example, in January 1935, when the National Committee of the French Socialist Party launched a program of *struggle for power, of destroying the bourgeois state apparatus, of instituting the democracy of the workers and peasants, of expropriating the banks and big industry.* (Program cited and approved by Trotsky. See *Whither France?*)

The revolutionary party formulates this program for the whole of the working class and for its government. We do not say: "Apply *our* program." We say: "A genuine workers' government which has effectively broken with the bourgeoisie will begin to apply this program" and will conduct an untiring propaganda around the transitional demands which constitute this program and which alone can concretize for the masses what *to break effectively with the bourgeoisie* means.

e) The formula of "workers' and farmers' government" is an inevitable consequence of the united front tactic, but not of a united front between the unions on a minimum basis of economic demands, but on a much higher basis, both political and economic, which embraces the highest domain of working class action, that of power.

f) A "C.P.-S.P.-C.G.T. government" applying *its* program in a parliamentary fashion is a bourgeois government, even if the whole of its members belong to a workers' party, as is the case with the present British Labour Party.

The revolutionary party does not *support*, does not *defend* these governments, not even for an instant, but on the contrary ought "to pitilessly unmask before the masses the true nature of these fake "workers' governments." (Resolution on Tactics, Fourth Congress of the C.I.)

g) The demand addressed to the traditional parties: "Break with the bourgeoisie, take power" should be accompanied not only by propaganda around the transitional demands which must constitute the program of the "workers' government," but also by propaganda along the following idea: A government of this kind is possible only by transcending the framework of bourgeois democracy, only by summoning the masses to revolutionary action, only by organizing them in formations suited to apply the working class program (committees of workers control over production, over food) and to combat the resistance of the bourgeoisie (militias).

It is not excluded that a "workers' government" can in exceptional conditions arise from a parliamentary combination. But what invests it with its effectively working class and anticapitalist character, is the program, the appeal to the masses, the organization of the masses.

At the same time the revolutionary party explains clearly to the masses that the formation of such a government will only be the first step along the road to the total overturn of the bourgeois state which can be accomplished only under the regime of the dictatorship of the proletariat.

The revolutionary party intends to lead the struggle for the formula of "workers' and farmers' government" as a slogan of current policy, concretized in each country in one or another manner, in this sense, and exclusively in this sense.

MAY 1946.

6. Report and discussion on the third Chinese revolution

The following are excerpts from a discussion that took place at the 11th Plenum of the International Executive Committee of the Fourth International in May, 1952. The discussion was inspired by a resolution on "The Third Chinese Revolution" written by Ernest Germain that had been adopted by the International Secretariat. The resolution, approved after the discussion at the plenum, was printed in the July–August 1952 issue of *Fourth International*, predecessor of *International Socialist Review*.

The resolution made three main contentions: (1) that the Third Chinese Revolution had established "a workers and peasants government" that would "only be a short, transitory stage along the road to the dictatorship of the proletariat"; (2) that the development of the revolution would assure the transformation of Mao's Communist party "from a highly opportunist workers party into a centrist party"; and (3) that the Fourth International should offer "critical support" to the new regime.

The views that a "workers and peasants government" had been established, and that the Chinese Communist party was a workers party, were challenged at the plenum, particularly by Peng Shu-tse, the central leader of the Chinese Trotskyists. On the question of the class character of Mao's party, Peng held that Trotsky's position that the Chinese CP was a Stalinist peasant party remained valid.

Ernest Germain was the reporter for the International Secretariat on this resolution. Those portions of the discussion dealing with the character of the new government appear below. They are reprinted from *SWP International Information Bulletin*, December 1952.

FROM 'REPORT ON THE CHINESE QUESTION' BY ERNEST GERMAIN

The character of the state and of the government

For after all, what we have seen up to now in the way of successive left turns in the policy of the Chinese CP will prove of lesser importance than the turns still ahead of us. The reason for this is simple: class contradictions are sharpening on the international level; they are sharpening on the national level. Opposing class forces will act with increasing violence, exercising an increasingly heavy pressure on the Chinese CP. The field for maneuver, the margin for conciliation and postponement is becoming increasingly contracted. The explosion of all the contradictions still enclosed in the policies of this party is thus becoming unavoidable.

The resolution which we are presenting for a vote at this Plenum strongly emphasizes the influence, which is already being exercised and which will be exercised all the more in the future, of the worldwide polarization of class forces on the course which the Chinese CP will pursue. The outbreak of the Korean war has already signalled an initial and violent offensive against the bourgeois formations which still remain in China. Is it at all conceivable that the Peoples Republic of China could tomorrow enter the third world war alongside the USSR and allow bourgeois property in the largest part of the industrial apparatus of the country to remain intact? The Chinese bourgeoisie knows that its only chance of salvation lies in a world victory of American imperialism. In the war between the USSR and China on one side and the imperialist powers on the other, it will not restrict itself to *desiring* the victory of the latter with all its heart. It would work practically and with all its means for this victory. It would be the most *defeatist* class toward the State of its "own" country that has been seen in the wars of the 20th century. It would sabotage the war economy, the industrial effort, supplying the war front. It is impossible that the Mao government should even allow so defeatist a class to retain control in the event of war, over the light industry of the country. Wholesale expropriation of the industrial bourgeoisie would inevitably follow on the outbreak of the third world war.

The polarization of class forces in China itself is moving no less rapidly toward such a final settling of accounts. In the editorial of *Peoples China* of March 15, 1952, devoted to the present movement "against waste, corruption and bureaucratism," Liu Tsun-chi writes that never have the capitalist private enterprises known such a prosperity in China as they are currently enjoying. "But to the same degree that these enterprises have developed and begun to flourish, the bourgeoisie has become less inclined to conform to the 'Common Program' and 'to obey governmental regulations'." Big capitalists have set up secret monopolies to control supplies to the State or to State enterprises. The forced concentration of enterprises and of capital has made rapid progress. Surprised, Liu Tsun-chi notes that the Chinese bourgeoisie has "used the same lamentable methods as are habitually used by big capitalists in the capitalist States" . . . The surprise is his alone. For us it is clear that the capitalists who are now collaborating with Mao's government have been doing so only out of considerations of the lesser evil or of immediate necessity, and not out of idealism or faith in the "Common Program." It was equally clear that precisely in the degree that Mao's policy tended toward stabilizing and enriching these private enterprises, that is to say, in the degree that the bourgeoisie again became rich, it would also become bolder, more determined to defend its own interests against the intrusion of the State into its private affairs, more inclined to intrude in its turn into State affairs, especially in the bureaucratic central State apparatus which became a bacteriological culture for all kinds of corruption.

The official authorities of the Chinese CP still declare, it is true, that the present struggle is directed solely against the "mangy sheep" of the bourgeoisie. But in the previously mentioned article in *Pravda* of April 23, 1952, Chen Po-ta expresses himself in the following way:

> Spurred by their hunger for profit, their inclination to speculation and to attaining advantages at the expense of others which is characteristic of the bourgeoisie, they (the capitalists) placed their agents in our state institutions and our public organizations, hired some of the employees of the State and of public bodies as their agents. Corruption on a very wide scale, concealment of income so as not to pay taxes, appropriation of state property . . . all that caused great damage. . . . Bourgeois elements did not give up their hope of conquering power bit by bit in the Peoples Republic of China, which is led by the great working class. They dreamed of delaying the preparations embarked on by the great Peoples Republic for passing over from the building of a peoples democracy onto the road of socialist development. . . . THE BOURGEOISIE IS STRIVING TO PUSH CHINA ONTO THE ROAD OF CAPITALISM. . . . But it is perfectly obvious that if the bourgeoisie persists in its efforts, it will meet with total defeat.

This analysis is on the whole accurate. Naturally, it does not mention the fact that bourgeois elements could "infiltrate" so easily into "our" State apparatus, because the latter, as is acknowledged in the *Peoples China* article mentioned previously, was taken over in its entirety in the big cities just as it was in the days of the Kuomintang. It does not mention the overwhelming responsibility of the leadership of the Chinese CP for this state of affairs, a leadership which could without any difficulty whatever have created a soviet China in 1949, even though it might have been necessary, for economic reasons, to retain large sectors of bourgeois property in light industry and in trade. But it is amply sufficient for us to observe: because of the nature of the Chinese CP, the central government of the Peoples Republic is not some kind of "neutral," subject to the "parallel" pressure of two opposing classes. *Fundamentally it acts and will act more and more*, under these pressures, *in the direction of completing the revolution*. We must be absolutely clear on this point if we do not want to meet up with new surprises and lose new opportunities for inscribing our movement in events.

But it is precisely for the same reason, because we are expecting these decisive left turns which are ahead of us, that we refrain for the moment from characterizing the Chinese State as a proletarian dictatorship. We repeat: it is not, by itself, the existence of bourgeois property in light industry and trade which restrains us. We have seen in Russia and could more readily expect to see in China the coexistence of a proletarian dictatorship with bourgeois property in large sectors of the economy. What restrains us is the twofold consideration of the structure of the State and the general dynamics of the revolution.

In large parts of China, notably in most of the provinces south of Yangtse, the Mao Tse-tung government has purely and simply taken over on its own account the old central administrations of the Kuomintang, including the very governors themselves. Only the armed power has been completely recast and represents an armed power with a different social character. State administration there has remained on the whole what it was before. Moreover, this involves the richest provinces in China, containing the center of light industry and of the bourgeoisie. The latter's representatives in the central government, even though they do not wield much power on the national level, represent useful observers for their class and are preparing positions for retaking power "bit by bit" as Chen Po-ta has said.

Naturally, this situation is not stable. On the morrow of the pacification of all of China, bourgeois power in the south was not only solidly entrenched in the cities, but equally well established in the villages, where the kulaks, as is confirmed by comrade Kim's report [see *SWP International Information Bulletin*, October 1952, "The Agrarian Reform in China," by Kim], had concentrated all power in their hands. With the development of agrarian reform, the *Peasant Associations* or associations of poor peasants have in many places practically conquered power and are exercising it like genuine soviets. These examples represent a magnificent agitational weapon for us. But they are not yet generalized to the point where we can say that the poor peasants exercise political power everywhere in the countryside. Nor, on the other hand, are they suppressing the duality of power, which factually exists in the measure that they must deal with the old apparatus, controlled by the class enemy, in the cities and administrative centers.

It is solely in the special conditions of this *State apparatus* that the bourgeois property which survives takes on an exceptional significance. For in this way it allows the bourgeoisie simultaneously to exert control from within, and to disintegrate and corrupt from without, the sectors of a new State apparatus which the Chinese CP is compelled to build.

The question becomes even clearer if we view the general march of the revolution. The latter has not been halted; it is not on the decline; its major surge is not behind but ahead of us. It is precisely the general attack against bourgeois property, the future and decisive left turn of the Chinese CP, which, by compelling the latter to mobilize the *city proletariat* on a vast scale for the first time, will mark the apogee of the revolution. If we state today that there is a proletarian dictatorship in China how would we characterize this decisive phase which lies ahead of us? How would we characterize the phase in which not only will the bourgeois representatives be truly eliminated from the central government and the old bourgeois State apparatus in the south destroyed, but in which undoubtedly and for the first time the proletariat will in action assert *as a class* its leading role in the revolution?

We leave not the slightest ambiguity as to the general direction in which the situation is evolving. We leave not the slightest ambiguity on the conscious role which the Chinese CP will play in these events. Nor do we leave the slightest ambiguity on the function which the central government of the Peoples Republic of China will fulfill. But we think that it is more prudent and more correct to stop at this point for the moment, to acknowledge the elements of dual power which still remain in China today, to characterize the government therefore as a workers and peasants government which has in practice already broken the coalition with the bourgeoisie and is rapidly advancing toward setting up the dictatorship of the proletariat.

PENG: . . . The main disagreement now lies in the characterization of the government. I think that it is an error to characterize the government as a workers and peasants government. I think that on the contrary our Chinese comrades could obtain an excellent response among the masses by launching the *slogan* of a workers and peasants government, that is to say, by *urging* the Chinese CP to break with the bourgeois parties, to halt all collaboration with the bourgeoisie and to exclude elements from the government. But we cannot conduct such an agitation if we say that the present government is already a workers and peasants government. . . .

CLAUDIO: I wish to point out the same error in formulation indicated by Comrade Dumas, as well as a passage on page 4 of the document, which gives the impression of jumping to a conclusion.

P. FRANK: Comrade Germain has correctly stressed the changes which the Chinese revolution has already effected in China itself. We had particularly stressed the international significance of the Chinese revolution at the Third World Congress, but this other aspect, its internal meaning for China, should have been emphasized more. When we see this movement that has projected a fourth of humanity so far ahead, we cannot in truth speak of a peasant revolt, for no peasant revolt brought that about. Most certainly it is the permanent revolution that is involved here. The enormous consequences of the conquest of power by Mao Tse-tung are sufficient for characterizing this movement as a *revolution* with a very great sweep.

It would be a serious error to undertake the characterization of the Chinese State with the same criteria which Trotsky used for characterizing the USSR. In the USSR we were confronted by the problems posed by the degeneration of a worker's state; in China we are confronted by the rising development of the revolution. Certainly this revolution starts from a very low level, lower even than the Russian revolution's, which was one of the lowest in the world. Moreover it starts under a leadership which is Stalinist by origin and education. But if we take the reality of China as our point of departure, we must understand that even under a Trotskyist leadership, it would have remained far from the norms. This does not do away with the need for criticizing the Chinese CP. But it does demand that we make only accurate criticisms, that is to say, those which take into account the objective conditions of China.

On the relationship between workers and peasants in the Chinese revolution, there is an interesting letter addressed by Trotsky in January 1931 to the Left Opposition. Some Chinese comrades had issued the slogan of "dictatorship of the proletariat and of the poor." Trotsky approved this and added that this slogan is not in the least in contradiction with the slogan of dictatorship of the proletariat, but on the contrary completes it. Trotsky added that we are for the dictatorship of the proletariat in China, but that we must understand that the proletariat represents a small minority in Chinese society, and that it can take power only if it groups the poor of the cities and countryside around itself.

Other comrades in China and in the International had developed erroneous ideas on the peasant armies. They considered these armies to have been mainly composed of lumpen elements. Trotsky, while admitting that lumpen elements slip into any insurgent army, underscored the fact that the overall peasant army has profound roots in the reality of the Chinese countryside and that it represents one of the principal elements on which the dictatorship of the proletariat will have to support itself.

While the resolution of the IS distinguishes between the present situation in China and the dictatorship of the proletariat, this is not so much because it involves differences in the political tasks to be resolved, but it does represent a difference in sociological definition. On this level, it is always preferable to be prudent. We were so, correctly, in the buffer zone regarding the going over toward a worker's state. And China is a vastly different country from Roumania! The process of revolutionary transformation there is enormous and is still far from being concluded. . . .

PABLO: . . . The difference between those who say that there is already a dictatorship of the proletariat in China and those who still speak of a workers and peasants government has to do with the evaluation of the stage reached at the present time by the Chinese revolution. The Chinese People's Republic was established at the time when the revolutionary army completed the conquest of the North. At that moment the bourgeois apparatus had not yet disintegrated in the South where the bourgeoisie was strongest. This apparatus has been purely and simply integrated into the new State apparatus. Its representatives sit in the central government. But this central government does not express the pressure of the bourgeoisie and that of the proletariat in an equal fashion. Proletarian preponderance there is clear, thanks to the leading role of the CP. However, in the South this preponderance does not as yet rest on a state apparatus controlled by the CP. There we have only a beginning of dual power. From this point of view, the revolution is only beginning in the South. But the dynamics of the national and international situation make the general and rapid destruction of this dual power in favor of proletarian power as the most probable, the almost certain variant. . . .

THEO: . . . From events, there are two essential points which must be grasped. The defeat of the Kuomintang sealed a decisive defeat of the bourgeoisie. In the perspectives which we have, the perspectives of war-revolution, this defeat must be considered as irreversible. Theoretically we could elaborate several possible variants. But to guide our immediate action, we can set aside all other variants and retain only that of the march toward the dictatorship of the proletariat. . . .

I am in agreement with the definition of the State and of the party as they are given in the resolution. The formula of a workers and peasants government appears to me the most satisfactory for the time being. . . .

BLEIBTREU: The action of the Communist Party in China and the reaction of the Kremlin have a great significance for us. Since 1946 the function of the Chinese CP is in opposition with the function of a CP controlled by the Kremlin in a period of inactivity of the masses, as is the case at present in France. When Mao goes to Moscow he is compelled to take different positions from those taken by Thorez because of the activity of the Chinese masses. That is why it is dangerous to draw automatic conclusions from the Chinese CP for other CP's.

The Chinese revolution is the main motor of the present world revolution. Its role is more direct in smashing imperialist positions than the totality of previous positions conquered by the working class. That is why we reject all characterizations such as military victory, peasant war, etc., used in conjunction with the triumph of Mao Tse-tung. The resolution uses unclear formulations in this connection. It speaks of the military victory of Mao, whereas what is involved is a revolution unleashed in 1946 and triumphing in 1949.

It is as a function of this historical analysis that the question of the State is posed. Therein lie two questions which cross each other and coincide: How does the permanent revolution start? How and when did the third Chinese revolution start? To speak of dual power, as the resolution does, answers nothing. A dual power in a State cannot remain symbolic. The remark that certain elements of dual power effectively exist is insufficient for setting aside the question of the character of the State. This question can be answered only as a function of a single decisive criterion: which class holds the essential elements of coercion? Germain has said: the role of the government is very unilateral. But he draws no conclusion from this observation in the resolution, insofar as the character of the State is concerned. The problem we are confronted with is precisely the meaning and function of this central government. If the resolution does not take a clear position on this question it is because it does not clearly characterize the mass movement since 1946 as a revolution and a civil war.

The discussion on the class character of the Chinese CP gives the answer to the question: which class holds the State power? The working class holds it through the CP as intermediary. In order to reestablish their power the former possessing classes cannot change the government through cold means. We can maintain that a return to former conditions in China would require a counterrevolution, a civil war. On the other hand, however, is it necessary to destroy the existing State in order to go ahead toward the solution of the tasks of the permanent revolution? Must a new State be built? Is a civil war necessary for that? It is by the road of reform that this can be realized, by very profound reforms of course. But the proletarian class struggle is not directed toward the destruction of the present State.

The question "which class holds the State power?" is a very important methodological question. The decisive criterion is not the question of nationalizations, but that of intervention by the masses. This factor is also a determinant in elaborating the perspectives of the Chinese CP. When the masses enter into struggle with such a sweep as they have in China, the CP ceases to be dependent on the Kremlin, ceases to be a Stalinist party in the classical meaning of the word....

JACQUES: I will vote against the resolution....

1. In characterizing the present regime in China, different confused formulations are used, which permit contradictory interpretations: dictatorship of the proletariat or dual power. What Bleibtreu has said on dual power is erroneous. A precondition for being able to speak of dual power is that the oppressed class has set up its own organs against the old State apparatus. That is the way things happened for example in Russia in 1917 with the Soviets. In China, the State apparatus is working for the bourgeoisie. Where is there anything in China which permits of a comparison with soviets?

We must see in what organs the working class finds expression as a class. In truth, the proletariat did not show itself as an active factor during the decisive events, as Comrade Peng has reported to us. The bourgeoisie was organized in the State of Chiang Kai-shek; it is organized today in the State of Mao. But where is the organization of the workers?

No more is it correct to speak of the government of Mao as a "workers and peasants government." In 1917, neither Lenin nor Trotsky gave that name to the Kerensky government. On the contrary they issued the slogan: "Throw out the capitalist ministers." But in China of today these capitalist ministers still continue in the government....

EXCERPTS FROM SUMMARY BY ERNEST GERMAIN

Once again on the class character of the state and of the government

Some very strange remarks have been made on this subject by Comrade Peng and Comrade Jacques. Comrade Jacques has compared the government of Mao with that of Kerensky. Comrade Peng has been of the opinion that we take away a weapon from the Chinese section by calling the Mao government a workers and peasants government, because, you see, our Chinese section should call for the establishment of such a workers and peasants government by expulsion of the capitalist ministers from the present government. Comrade Peng has even found a contradiction in what we say, because, he says, we admitted that in 1929, when the CP advocated the establishment of soviets and of a workers and peasants government, it was a peasant party, and today, when there is no question either of soviets or of a workers and peasants government, but only of the "new democracy," we call it a workers party....

All this reasoning bears the hallmark of absolutely mechanistic and formalistic thought.

It is not because certain gentlemen in black frock coats commonly termed bourgeois sat in his government that Kerensky was Kerensky. It was because, at the order and in the service of these gentlemen, he prevented agrarian reform, allowed free rein to the speculation and economy-strangling maneuvers of the capitalists, and plotted in the corridors with the Russian Chiang Kai-shek, named Kornilov or Krasnov, to drown the power of the workers and peasants in blood. Mao Tse-tung, on the contrary has smashed the power of the Chinese Kornilovs, Krasnovs and Kerensky's by crushing them militarily, supported by the overwhelming majority of the poor peasants and with the sympathy, at any rate, of the overwhelming majority of the proletariat. He has not prevented but has carried out agrarian reform. He has not safeguarded but has seriously restricted the "freedom of speculation" and of profit of the capitalists. He has not reversed but has advanced, developed, and accelerated the revolutionary process. Isn't it an aberration, under these conditions, to compare him to Kerensky, supporting oneself solely on the fact that there are several bourgeois in his government, without asking oneself what is the power of these bourgeois, without posing the question: "Who controls, who rules whom?" . . .

In 1932, in the full ebb-tide of the revolution, the CP found its forces isolated in the countryside. Trotsky was absolutely correct in indicating the danger of the infiltration of petty-bourgeois ideology into the CP, the danger of corruption by this milieu and by this ideology under the concrete conditions of defeat and isolation. These conditions were infinitely more important in determining the physiognomy of the party than radical phrases about soviets and a workers and peasants government, which influenced nobody anyway. Today, the CP, carried ahead by an overwhelming sweep of the revolution, has been compelled to crush the central power of the bourgeoisie and to carry out the agrarian reform, thereby in practice breaking with the bourgeoisie and in practice realizing the workers and peasants government. This practice is infinitely more important in determining the present physiognomy of this party than reactionary and deceptive phrases about the "bloc of 4 classes" and the "new democracy." Only those who judge the policies of a party by its words and not by its acts can say under these conditions that the policies of Mao remain "fundamentally the same." For us, an abyss separates these policies from those of the past. This abyss was hewed out by a colossal fact: the revolution, the revolutionary action of tens of millions of poor peasants!

Bleibtreu commits a mechanistic and formalistic error similar to that of Comrades Peng and Jacques. Must the bourgeoisie make a counterrevolution to reestablish its power? he asks. Yes. Must the proletariat make a revolution to complete the realization of the revolutionary tasks? No. Therefore, we are confronting a workers State. Bleibtreu forgets a little thing: that the struggle between the revolution and counterrevolution *is still taking place*, that the civil war of the bourgeoisie of which he speaks is not a thing of the future *but is now unfolding in China*. That is what we are talking about when we say that the permanent revolution is unfolding before our eyes in this immense country. When you try to apply the categories of formal logic to movement, mistakes are inevitable. When you try to apply to a situation of civil war, of revolution in process but not yet completed, the criteria used for judging the nature of established, recognized, stable states, mistakes are equally inevitable. On the level of the central government, two governments do not confront each other in China, as was the case in Russia, or in Germany in 1918, or in Spain, at least in an embryonic form, in 1936. But read the report of Comrade Kim to find out what the situation is in the villages, the cantons, the provinces of the south. A veritable civil war is raging there, whose existence moreover is conceded by the central authorities since they speak of thousands of "bandits" who are periodically "wiped out" and who are mobilized in defense of the landlords. And who holds the power in the cities and in the capitals themselves in the southern provinces? In numerous cases, it is the old leaders of the Kuomintang, that is to say, the representatives of the village bourgeoisie and of the landlords. Who holds power in the villages after the realization of agrarian reform? The peasant associations and poor peasant associations, who are factually functioning like genuine soviets. Do we have dual power there or don't we when city and village confront each other in this way? Is there a civil war there in which *for the time being* the state power of the old classes has not as yet been completely liquidated but is to have its fate sealed by the outcome of the struggle itself? Regarding the outcome of this struggle, no doubt exists, neither for us nor for Bleibtreu. Thanks to the "unilateral" role of the central government and of the peoples army, the old possessing classes will be crushed. But this does not yet justify, in analysing the facts as they exist, that we, today, jump over this stage of their subsequent and final destruction, and consider as already existing what will come into being in a year or two. . . .

Excerpt from final remarks

I am in agreement with the proposals of Comrades Dumas and Claudio.[4] As for the Bleibtreu amendments, a series of them which involve only questions of formulation can be accepted by us. Bleibtreu has used a great deal of time and energy to sharpen nonexistent differences artificially. We know as well as he does that there has been an enormous revolution in China and not a military campaign. The only difference between us is regarding the evaluation of the present stage attained by this revolution. . . .

---

4. The following footnote appeared in the *International Information Bulletin* from which these excerpts are taken: Comrade Dumas took the floor to point out the need, in his opinion, of changing the formulation of two passages on pages 2 and 6 of the proposed resolution, which might give the impression that a dictatorship of the proletariat already exists.

7. The Algerian revolution from 1962 to 1969

The following resolution was passed by the December 1969 Plenum of the International Executive Committee of the Fourth International. The document explains how the "workers and peasants government" that the Fourth International held had come to power in Algeria stagnated and went into decline rather than moving toward the overthrow of capitalism as did the "workers and peasants government" in Cuba. A letter by Joseph Hansen on this topic appears in the preceding section of this collection.

The resolution is reprinted from the March 16, 1970 issue of *Intercontinental Press*, a revolutionary Marxist international newsweekly and news service.

I

Six months after the coup d'etat that overthrew Ahmed Ben Bella, the Eighth World Congress of the Fourth International, meeting in December 1965, analyzed the situation in Algeria in a resolution, "Progress and Problems of the African Revolution." This analysis singled out the following aspects in the development of the Algerian revolution from 1954 to 1965:

1. Before independence, the Algerian revolution took the form of a deep-going mobilization of the masses. The political instrument of the revolution, the FLN [Front de Libération Nationale—National Liberation Front], took form as a politically ill-defined multiclass front.

2. Following independence, the FLN literally burst into fragments at the time of the crisis in the summer of 1962, which developed along very unclear lines.

3. A new stage, characterized by a dynamic of growing over into socialism, opened with the exodus of the French *colons*. The rising curve in the revolution reached its highest point with the March 1963 decrees and continued up to the expropriation measures in October of the same year. Observing this process, the United Secretariat of the Fourth International took note of the fact that a workers and peasants government had been established in Algeria. At that time the process had already slowed and a pause had set in.

4. Algerian society remained marked by the coexistence and conflict of different and antagonistic forces and sectors. A significant Algerian private capitalist sector continued to exist, including in the countryside, as well as a powerful foreign capitalist sector (oil and gas). Furthermore, imperialist aid continued to be important and Algeria remained dependent on the franc zone. An administrative, economic, and military state bureaucracy developed which enjoyed a privileged share of the national income.

5. The coup d'etat of June 19, 1965, was the outcome of the deterioration in the situation which Ben Bella could no longer forestall. The coup d'etat was supported by the most well-known representative of the state and army bureaucracy. Its result was to encourage those forces most hostile to a socialist conclusion to the Algerian revolution.

In adopting these conclusions, the world congress, however, left discussion open on the Algerian question.

II

Immediately after June 19, 1965, two factors favored a temporary misunderstanding of the nature of the coup d'etat and some hesitation among the revolutionary vanguard in designating the character of the Boumédienne regime.

(a) The fact that the coup eliminated only a relatively small number of figures, while a whole series of ministers in the Ben Bella government joined Boumédienne's "Council of the Revolution."

(b) The support which the Chinese leadership gave to the Boumédienne regime in the weeks following the coup and which was motivated by considerations of a factional nature linked to the way in which Ben Bella and his team had been preparing the Afro-Asian conference.

Today these factors are no longer operative. The nature of the Boumédienne government became clear to the revolutionary vanguard when Boumédienne adopted a completely different orientation from that of the Ben Bella government.

Other changes should be noted. Moscow, and not Peking, is making conciliatory moves toward the regime, accompanying this with an attempt on the ideological level to paint up the Boumédienne regime as "anti-imperialist." This line is being followed by the PAGS [Parti de l'Avant-garde Socialiste—Socialist Vanguard party, formerly ORP (Organisation de la Résistance Populaire—People's Resistance Organization) founded after June 19] in which former members of the Parti Communiste Algérien [PCA—Algerian Communist party] are active. In addition, after the Algerian leaders assumed verbal "leftist" positions in the Israeli-Arab conflict, Fidel Castro, who had very severely condemned the authors of the coup d'etat, went back on his condemnation, doing this in the form of self-criticism.

In view of possible confusion from these sources, it is necessary to reaffirm the position of the revolutionary Marxists on the present regime in Algeria without any ambiguities.

The June 19 coup d'etat marked the destruction of the workers and peasants government. The molecular changes for the worse, which had been accumulating both in the consciousness of the various classes and in the government personnel and organization, had ended in a qualitative change. Having seized power with relative ease, owing to the previous deterioration in the situation, Boumédienne and his army had little trouble in putting down the opposition. The new power represented a reactionary resolution of the contradiction that had existed between the capitalist state and the workers and peasants government with its socialist orientation.

In the following period extending from 1965 to the end of 1967, there was an increasing drift to the right although centers of resistance still remained. At the end of 1967, a second period opened, which continues to the present, with the rise of Kaïd Achmed (former Commander Slimane) to the second highest political post in the country, the position of head of the "party."

In this shift, a dual phenomenon should be noted:

(a) The development of a state capitalist sector in the economy in close osmosis with imperialist interests.

(b) The steady loss of momentum by the UGTA [Union Générale des Travailleurs Algériens—General Union of Algerian Workers] trade-union apparatus. This apparatus thought it could maintain its independence and serve as a center for a new mobilization of the masses by limiting itself in the interval to a defensive struggle to preserve self-management, if not to a purely economic struggle.

The attempted counter coup d'etat of El Affroun, led by Tahar Zbiri in December 1967 and supported by a section of the trade-union militants, was a desperate attempt to reverse the trend to the right. The masses did not intervene in any way.

III

The essential feature in the changes which have occurred in the Algerian economic structure has been the strengthening of the "mixed" (state capitalism and foreign capital) fuels sector of the Algerian economy. This is the main sector of the economy from the standpoint of export and has undergone constant expansion (39,700,000 tons produced in 1967 as against 26,100,000 in 1964). The fuels sector is dominated by Sonatrach [Société Nationale Algérienne pour la Recherche, la Production, la Transformation et la Commercialisation des Hydrocarbures—National Algerian Company for Research, Production, Conversion, and Sale of Hydrocarbons], a state company which was created originally to manage the third Hassi Messaoud-Arzew pipeline completed in 1966 but which has developed into one of the principal petroleum producers. The activities of Sonatrach, which is aided by American and Soviet experts and collaborates closely with foreign interests, have expanded to such a degree that this enterprise constitutes a veritable state within a state. The basis for the collaboration between imperialism and the state sector is still the 1965 oil agreement concluded shortly after the June 19 coup d'etat and ratified in the French parliament by a UNR-PCF [Union pour la Nouvelle République-Parti Communiste Français—Union for the New Republic (the Gaullist party)—French Communist party] majority. Algerian state capitalism has been collaborating with imperialism without any major conflicts. The "nationalization" of the American oil companies' distribution network in September 1967 was, in appearance, an anti-imperialist measure in response to the Israeli aggression. In reality it was a purchase agreed to by the companies involved. The same was true of the purchase of the other distribution centers in May 1968. While collaborating with imperialism, the state sector seeks to assure its control over the transfer of currency and to impose its conditions with regard to export prices. These are minor conflicts in which the primary objective is "getting into position" for the renewal of the 1965 agreement in 1969.

It must be added that the Algerian left forces have never advanced specific demands for this sector, limiting themselves to declaring that nationalization of mineral and energy resources was a "long-term goal" (1964 *Algiers Charter*).

As against the constant expansion of this sector, the modest self-managed industrial sector, composed in general of old plants, is steadily losing momentum. Its social weight is minimal. The workers in this sector are calculated at less than 15,000 (6 percent of the Algerian working class). Moreover, the new investment code freezes the limit of development of this sector. It guarantees that there will be no nationalization of the foreign capital invested in Algeria for ten years' time and that after that it can be nationalized only with payment of 100 percent compensation.

The nationalization of the French plants in June 1968, planned by American and Swiss "experts," was carried out according to this schema. These plants were turned over to state companies that were not self-managed. Some of them were previously self-managed plants returned to their former owners (Norcolor). In other cases, the "nationalization-purchase" was made long after these concerns had brought the enterprises in the self-managed industrial sector to their knees (oil works, soap factories).

Parallel to the industrial sector, peasant self-management has had to struggle constantly against sabotage by the authorities combined with difficulties on the French wine market (wine import quotas).

As for the "agrarian reform," adopted in 1966 but left unimplemented, it itself is nothing but a caricature of the reform drawn up under the Ben Bella government. Matching the appetites of the state bureaucracy, it is limited to an area producing a net annual income equal to the state payroll.

IV

In Algeria the bourgeoisie was exceptionally weak both socially and politically. It lacked the capacity to meet the revolution head-on at this stage. The immediate source, therefore, of the counterrevolutionary initiatives was the state bureaucracy.

In order to understand the reasons for the behavior of this new bureaucracy, we must examine the elements making it up, its international context, and the international social forces on which it bases itself.

We can define three layers in the Algerian state bureaucracy. These layers are based on the social interests they have represented in post-1962 Algeria, independently of the social origins of the bureaucrats themselves. According to this criterion, a bureaucrat may drift imperceptibly from one stratum to another.

1. A layer that made it possible to maintain a "well functioning" state apparatus between the cease-fire and the formation of the first Ben Bella government. It is composed of a certain number of functionaries, who were former or recent col-

laborators of the colonial regime, coming from the famous "Lacoste promotion." It is made up both of Algerians and reformed and cooperative *pieds-noirs* [French persons born in Algeria]. This stratum is the most faithful supporter of the leaders who want to maintain a state of the bourgeois type. By its inertia and its sabotage of revolutionary measures, this layer plays an important braking role. It hides behind the mask of "technical competence" in order to maintain itself. But it is being subjected to criticism by the most conscious cadres, who demand that it be purged. The continually promised removal of this stumbling block is always indefinitely postponed. This stratum takes advantage of the delay to consolidate its privileges and it exercises a pernicious influence on the opportunistic nationalist cadres who are slipping into reactionary positions.

2. The national bourgeoisie was extensively represented in the first Ben Bella government. These cadres based themselves in the state apparatus on a bureaucratic layer of high functionaries (cabinet members, prefects) whose actions then and since have been guided by the same class interests. Khider, the secretary of the FLN, worked in the party apparatus to consolidate the power of these strata, if not for a seizure of power by them. Representatives of this layer were to be found in the successive Ben Bella governments. A few were unmasked, but these bourgeois bureaucrats remained throughout the machinery of state. Certain bourgeois technocrats remain also in the Boumédienne government.

3. The third layer in the state bureaucracy, and the most numerous, formed as a bureaucratic layer in the FLN administrative apparatus during the war. It emerged from the agrarian and urban petty bourgeoisie which flocked to the FLN and the ALN [Armée de Libération Nationale—National Liberation Army]. This layer rallied first to Ben Bella and then to Boumédienne. It includes the majority of the army and men in the ministries whose opposition to the June 1968 "nationalizations" tends to show that some of them, too, have slipped into the first group. The vast majority of the intermediate-level functionaries in the ministries and the local administrations have come from different strata of the petty bourgeoisie—small and middle tradesmen, middle peasants, petty functionaries of the colonial era. The ANP [Armée Nationale Populaire—National People's Army] officers are almost entirely representatives of the petty bourgeoisie.

A part of this stratum came from the working class in the cities or in emigration. Former working-class cadres in the MTLD [Mouvement pour le Triomphe des Libertés Démocratiques—Movement for the Achievement of Democratic Liberties] and former CGT [Confédération Générale du Travail—General Confederation of Labor] or UGTA unionists have risen to positions of responsibility in the state apparatus. Boumaza, Alia Yahia, and Zerdani represented this element. But in the context of the alliance that the petty bourgeoisie has concluded with the national bourgeoisie, this layer of the working-class bureaucracy, which is rather weak, has vacillated between the government and the masses to the extent that it experiences the political pressure of the masses. This layer will never be capable (with very rare exceptions) of conducting a proletarian policy. It is being totally rooted out of the state apparatus.

The most characteristic feature of this state bureaucracy is its heterogeneity. Representatives of the national bourgeoisie are found side by side with representatives of the working class, in the same ministerial and government commissions, in the Political Bureau.

The question which arises continually for each of these strata is, whom to serve. Such a heterogeneous bureaucracy becomes conscious of its social role only through constant confrontation with the social forces and classes which it claims to serve as a whole. This is why since 1962 all government bodies have been torn by clique infighting and struggles over immediate interests.

The pressures of imperialism on this bureaucracy must not be overlooked. French imperialism has brought pressure to bear through economic cooperation, continuation of the Evian accords, and the 1965 hydrocarbon agreements; British imperialism through mixed companies. American imperialism has exercised pressure through its not inconsiderable economic aid. And West German imperialism as well as others have been present. No less important is the considerable economic aid provided by the bureaucracies of the workers states—the USSR, China, and Yugoslavia heading the list. Far from being provided in accordance with the principles proclaimed by Che Guevara at the Algiers Afro-Asian Economic Seminar, this aid has been accompanied by declarations favorable to the regimes in power and in the last analysis has favored stabilization of the state structures and the status quo. The same effect was produced by the ideological default of the former PCA (especially in the newspaper *Alger Républicain*) and later, after Harbi's arrest, of the ORP-PAGS which assumed that a "socialist state" or a "non-capitalist road" had been achieved or was in the process of being achieved (and still speculating, even today, on conflicts in top government circles).

Enmeshed in this international context, the state bureaucratic structures have become allied with the retrograde social forces.

V

The general political resolution of the Second Congress of the UGTA in 1965 pointed to the "bureaucratic layer being formed" among the "forces of counterrevolution," alongside the feudalists and exploitative bourgeoisie.

But the Oumeziane leadership of the UGTA, elected at the Second Congress, timidly avoided drawing the necessary conclusions from this analysis. It tried to counter the dismantlement of self-management by a defensive struggle, seeking support in the government. Its paper has been repeatedly prevented from coming out (May 1966, December 1967, and up to the present).

In Algeria today, the workers' right to determine the rules under which their unions function, to elect their representatives freely, to formulate their program without interference from the authorities, and to decide their actions in complete independence—that is, the four necessary criteria of trade-union independence from the state apparatus—has been deprived of all semblance of reality.

VI

At the present time, despite Cherif Belkacem's and then Kaïd Achmed's "reorganization," the "FLN party" is still nonexistent.

But on the side of the opposition organizations, the picture is not a reassuring one.

(a) The CNDR [Conseil National de la Révolution—National Council of the Revolution] or ex-PRS [Parti de la Révolution Socialiste—Party of the Socialist Revolution] was never able to develop after its initial "Menshevik-type" positions condemning the Ben Bella government's revolutionary measures as "premature."

(b) The PAGS or ex-ORP became nothing but a vehicle of the Kremlin's foreign policy, under Alleg's leadership after Mohammed Harbi and Sahouane were arrested. This was shown by its turn on January 26, 1966, toward the formation of a broad "people's democratic" front demanding even the release of Ait Ahmed, who was imprisoned at that time, and proposing a front with the FFS [Front des Forces Socialistes—Front of Socialist Forces]. It has no mass base.

(c) Ait Ahmed's FFS and Mohamed Labjaoui's OCRA [Organisation Clandestine de la Révolution Algérienne—Clandestine Organization of the Algerian Revolution] represent factions in the bourgeois and petty-bourgeois wing of the old apparatuses.

(d) The RUR [Rassemblement Unitaire des Révolutionnaires—Movement to Unite Revolutionists], which was born of splits from the ex-ORP and the OCRA, represents, from the standpoint of its program and its analyses, the tendency closest to revolutionary socialism. Its base in Algeria, however, is as limited as that of the other movements.

VII

1. In this context the fundamental strategic task remains the organization of a revolutionary Marxist vanguard and the subsequent formation of a party of the urban and rural workers which would struggle for the overthrow of the Boumédienne regime and the establishment of a government of the worker and peasant masses.

2. Inseparably bound up with this task is the necessity of struggling to revitalize the trade-union movement and gain its complete independence from the state.

3. This struggle can only be waged through and parallel to a revival of the mass movement. And the mass movement can be revived only through struggle for:

(a) Stimulation of the noncapitalist sector of the economy by putting the entire nationalized industrial sector under self-management and giving priority to this sector as regards fiscal advantages and the development of trade relations, etc.

(b) The establishment of a monopoly of foreign trade and the introduction of mandatory national planning to avert strangulation of the self-managed sector.

(c) Nationalization of the petroleum-producing enterprises belonging to all the imperialist countries involved in the June 1967 aggression against the Arab revolution, and the establishment of workers control exercised jointly by representatives of the oil workers and the socialist industrial sector over Sonatrach and the other oil companies.

(d) Abrogation of the pseudo-agrarian reform of 1966 and implementation of a radical agrarian reform by means of expropriation of the large landowners and severe limitations on the right to hold property in land. The starting consideration must be that it is of course incorrect to call only for the restriction of large and middle landownership independent of seeking the most productive use of the land. But it is not correct either to envisage agrarian reform as an attempt to put the most land possible under cultivation according to abstract criteria of economic efficiency, independent of social relationships.

(e) Amendment of the 1966 law on municipal government for a new definition of municipal boundaries guaranteeing that the municipalities will be economic units and eliminating interference by the FLN apparatus.

(f) Defense of the revolution by the creation of workers and peasants militias based on the big farms, the big factories, and the municipalities.

(g) Renovation and purging of the state apparatus, the creation of organs of people's power, and promotion of equalitarian tendencies in the struggle against bureaucratic privileges. Revival of the struggle for democratic demands—emancipation of women, the struggle to keep Islam out of public affairs, the struggle against illiteracy and for education, the struggle against regional particularism.

4. Particular importance must be accorded to work among the Algerian workers in Europe as well as work for the release of all the interned militants and leaders, especially Ben Bella, Ben Allah, Zahouane, Harbi, and Hadj Ali.

VIII

Today the Trotskyist movement is unanimous in its assessment of the current situation in Algeria. After the June 19 coup d'etat, however, the limited extent of the change in the government makeup led some militants to ask whether the character of this coup had not been exaggerated; since, after all, it did not exceed the dimensions of a palace revolution. Subsequently the majority agreed that the coup was the qualitative expression of a molecular deterioration which had occurred in the last period of President Ben Bella's regime. But in view of the rapidity with which the state bureaucracy accentuated its right turn, a second question arose: Did the Trotskyist movement exaggerate the advances of the Algerian revolution in February 1964 when it characterized the Ben Bella government as a workers and peasants government? This is the question that must be answered now.

There is no reason to minimize the real advances that marked the development of the Algerian revolution during the first years after independence. Real anti-imperialist and anticapitalist actions were taken by the Ben Bella government and, more precisely, the limited team around Ben Bella, which in important instances went beyond the institutional framework, legalizing the conquests of the masses by decrees. The Fourth International was correct in giving critical support to the Ben Bella team from the time it conquered power in July 1962.

It is, however, likewise necessary to take into account the fact that the masses in movement who won self-management were the permanent workers on the large estates that later became self-managed farms; that is, the agricultural proletariat in the true sense of the word. After the summer of 1962, this agricultural proletariat was the only sector of the masses in motion. This was the social base of the Ben Bella team. Its relative narrowness constituted a most serious weakness. The masses of poor peasants could have offered a broader social base, but they were atomized during the crises of the summer of 1962. They could have been mobilized through immediate implementation of a radical agrarian reform. But the Ben Bella team did not do this.

The Fourth International did not correctly estimate the narrowness of the social base on which the Ben Bella team rested and therefore failed to see the major difference between the situation in Algeria and the situation which led to the establishment of a workers state in Cuba less than two years after the Castroist team took power.

In this situation, a revolutionary leadership possessing an adequate instrument, a revolutionary party, could still have mobilized the peasant masses. But in Algeria, the FLN was never a "party" in the class sense. Moreover, it no longer existed after 1958, except as an organization in the federation of France and as a government in the GPRA [Gouvernement Provisoire de la République Algérienne—Provisional Government of the Algerian Republic]. For all other purposes it had abdicated in favor of the ALN.

In its early stages, the Algerian freedom struggle had served as an inspiring example throughout the colonial world. The Cubans, especially, were influenced by it. After the victory of the Cuban revolution and the establishment first of a workers and peasants government and then a workers state in Cuba, this reciprocal influence continued, with Cuba now becoming an example for the Algerians. It was legitimate in Algeria to hold up the example of Cuba and to struggle for a similar outcome.

However, the dynamics of the Algerian revolution was determined by important differences from the developments that led to the establishment of the Cuban workers state. French imperialism had drawn a lesson from the victory of the Cuban revolution; it followed a different course from the one taken by U.S. imperialism toward Castro. The mass mobilizations were much more limited in Algeria than in Cuba. The Ben Bella team was of much lower revolutionary political stature than the Castro-Guevara team in Cuba. It failed especially to smash all surviving elements of the bourgeois army—which in Cuba were smashed upon Castro's entering Havana. Instead, in accordance with one of the main provisions of the Evian agreement, Ben Bella allowed these elements to be integrated into the ALN. In view of these differences, which became evident in the course of the struggle, it was a mistake to expect an outcome analogous to the one in Cuba.

This error in estimate was made worse by a wrong assessment of the nature of the ALN, especially after the application of the Evian agreement, and by the conception, maintained primarily by the Pablo tendency, that in the concrete Algerian situation of 1962–63 the army could play the role of the party. The grave consequences of the delay in organizing an Algerian revolutionary vanguard were seriously underestimated.

The Pablo tendency, which was in charge of the work in Algeria and which also controlled the journal of the French section of the Fourth International for at least two years, tended to develop its own independent line. It advanced confused and incorrect formulas with regard to the Algerian state, calling it an "anticapitalist state" or "semi-workers state." It did not grasp the contradiction between the workers and peasants government and the bourgeois character of the state apparatus. It therefore assigned to mass mobilizations essentially the role of supporting the Ben Bella tendency and carrying out the program of the FLN, failing to appreciate that it was crucial for the urban and rural proletariat and poor peasantry to set up independent organs of power, and clinging to the utopian and non-Marxist concept of the possibility of a gradual change in the nature of the state.

From this, various consequences followed such as minimizing certain serious events; for example, the gangster-like attack committed by the Khider apparatus at the UGTA congress, which was explained away by calling the UGTA leaders "left Mensheviks."

The Pablo tendency eventually split from the Fourth International.

The Fourth International never used the category of workers and peasants government in the Algerian context as a synonym for a dictatorship of the proletariat. The state structure was always correctly analyzed as bourgeois.

But although the International correctly applied the designation of workers and peasants government to the Ben Bella regime, it did not sufficiently stress the imperious necessity of establishing independent organs of political power by the urban and rural proletariat. Such bodies, moreover, would have been the best instruments for a general mobilization of the masses and the sole means for making the process of permanent revolution irreversible.

A concomitant error was committed in May 1964 when the International Executive Committee set the task for the revolutionary Marxists of collaborating in the formation of a revolutionary socialist left "led by the FLN" (the IEC resolution, "The International Situation and the Tasks of the Revolutionary Marxists," *Quatriéme Internationale*, July 1964) instead of stressing the need to work among the ranks first to create a revolutionary Marxist organization linked to the Algerian masses.

The lesson of the events in Algeria is of considerable importance. The victory of the socialist revolution in Algeria was possible. But a decisive factor was lacking: the revolutionary party.

Within the frame of this self-criticism it must be added frankly that if the participation of the Trotskyist movement in the Algerian revolution, including its material support to the struggle and its backing of the most progressive tendency after 1962, was considerable, too little was done in carrying out the specific function of the Trotskyist movement—to form the nucleus of a future Algerian revolutionary party. The work of training and recruiting Algerian militants was neglected for work at the top.

Doubtless, during an initial phase, in view of the smallness of our forces, it was correct to concentrate on a campaign of practical support for the revolution which was creating a climate favorable to the spread of our ideas. But after a given point, the formation of an organized nucleus should have been given priority and all work at the top subordinated to this goal. The International recognized this at its Sixth World Congress. It did not, however, make the necessary effort to carry out this line. Thus, it shares the blame for this error with the comrades of the Pablo tendency, who were the main ones responsible for this work and for the false orientation as regards building a revolutionary nucleus.

Also from Pathfinder

The Communist Manifesto
Karl Marx and Frederick Engels

Communism, say the founding leaders of the revolutionary workers movement, is not a set of ideas or preconceived "principles" but workers' line of march to power, springing from a "movement going on under our very eyes." $5. Also in Spanish, French, Farsi, and Arabic.

Socialism: Utopian and Scientific
Frederick Engels

"To make men the masters of their own form of social organization—to make them free—is the mission of the modern proletariat," writes Engels. A classic guide to the operations of capitalism and struggles of the working class. $10. Also in Farsi.

The Teamster Series
Farrell Dobbs

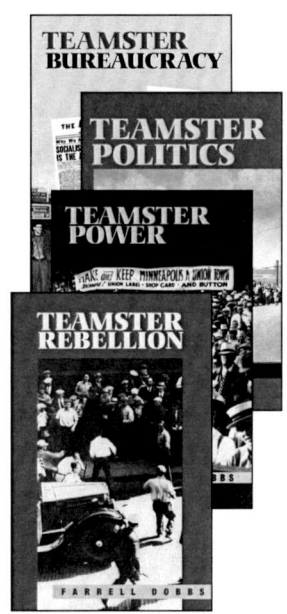

"The principal lesson from the Teamster experience is not that, under an adverse relationship of forces, the workers can be overcome, but that, with proper leadership, they can overcome." —*Farrell Dobbs*

Four books on the strikes, organizing drives, and political campaigns that transformed the Teamsters across the Midwest in the 1930s into a militant industrial union movement. Written by the general organizer of these Teamster battles and leader of the Socialist Workers Party.

A tool for workers seeking to use union power in every workplace and advance the fight for an independent labor party. $16 each, series $50. Also in Spanish.
Teamster Rebellion is available in French, Farsi, and Greek.

Art and Revolution
WRITINGS ON LITERATURE, POLITICS, AND CULTURE
Leon Trotsky

"Art can become a strong ally of revolution only insofar as it remains faithful to itself," wrote Trotsky in 1938. $15

New International
A MAGAZINE OF MARXIST POLITICS AND THEORY

CAPITALISM'S LONG HOT WINTER HAS BEGUN
JACK BARNES

Today's global capitalist crisis is but the opening stage of decades of economic, financial, and social convulsions and class battles. Class-conscious workers confront this historic turning point for imperialism with confidence, Jack Barnes writes, drawing satisfaction from being "in their face" as we chart a revolutionary course to take power. In *New International* no. 12. $14. Also in Spanish, French, Farsi, Arabic, and Greek.

OUR POLITICS START WITH THE WORLD
JACK BARNES

The huge economic and cultural inequalities between imperialist and semicolonial countries, and among classes within them, are accentuated by the workings of capitalism. To build parties able to lead a successful revolutionary struggle for power in our own countries, vanguard workers must be guided by a strategy to close this gap. In *New International* no. 13. $14. Also in Spanish, French, Farsi, and Greek.

IMPERIALISM'S MARCH TOWARD FASCISM AND WAR
JACK BARNES

"There will be new Hitlers, new Mussolinis. That is inevitable. What is not inevitable is that they will triumph. The working-class vanguard will organize our class to fight back against the devastating toll we are made to pay for the capitalist crisis. The future of humanity will be decided in the contest between these contending class forces." In *New International* no. 10. $14. Also in Spanish, French, Farsi, and Greek.

The Jewish Question
A MARXIST INTERPRETATION
Abram Leon

Why is Jew-hatred still raising its ugly head? What are its class roots—from antiquity through feudalism, to capitalism's rise and current crises? Why is there no solution under capitalism? The author, Abram Leon, was killed in the Nazi gas chambers. Revised translation, new introduction, and 40 pages of illustrations and maps. $17. Also in Spanish and French.

Puerto Rico: Independence Is a Necessity
Rafael Cancel Miranda

One of the five Puerto Rican Nationalists imprisoned by Washington for more than 25 years and released in 1979 speaks out on the brutal reality of US colonial domination, the example of Cuba's socialist revolution, and the ongoing struggle for independence. $5. Also in Spanish and Farsi.

Are They Rich Because They're Smart?
CLASS, PRIVILEGE, AND LEARNING UNDER CAPITALISM
Jack Barnes

Exposes growing class inequalities in the US and the self-serving rationalizations of well-paid professionals who think their "brilliance" equips them to "regulate" working people, who don't know what's in our own best interest. $10. Also in Spanish, French, Farsi, and Arabic.

February 1965: The Final Speeches
Malcolm X

Our revolt is not "simply a racial conflict of Black against white, or a purely American problem. Rather, we are seeing a global rebellion of the oppressed against the oppressor, the exploited against the exploiter." Speeches and interviews from the last three weeks of Malcolm X's life. $17

WWW.PATHFINDERPRESS.COM

EXPAND YOUR REVOLUTIONARY LIBRARY

Labor, Nature, and the Evolution of Humanity
The Long View of History
FREDERICK ENGELS, KARL MARX, GEORGE NOVACK, MARY-ALICE WATERS

Why is it important to know that social labor, transforming nature, has been the motor force of humanity's evolution for millions of years? Because without that knowledge, working people are unable to see beyond the capitalist epoch, beyond the class exploitation that warps all human relations, ideas, and values. The dictatorship of capital had a beginning . . . and it will have an end. But only the revolutionary conquest of state power by the working class can open the door to a world free of capitalism's dog-eat-dog social reality. A world built on human solidarity. A socialist world. $12. Also in Spanish and French.

Thomas Sankara Speaks
The Burkina Faso Revolution, 1983–87

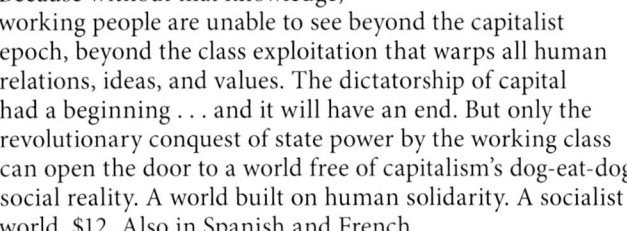

Under Sankara's guidance, Burkina Faso's revolutionary government led peasants, workers, women, and youth to expand literacy; to sink wells, plant trees, erect housing; to combat women's oppression; to carry out land reform; to join others worldwide to free themselves from the imperialist yoke. $20. Also in French.

Women's Liberation and the African Freedom Struggle
THOMAS SANKARA

"There is no true social revolution without the liberation of women," explains the leader of the 1983–87 revolution in the West African country of Burkina Faso. $5. Also in Spanish, French, and Farsi.

Leon Trotsky on France
An assessment of the social and economic crisis that shook France in the mid-1930s in the aftermath of Hitler's rise to power in Germany, and a program to unite the working class and exploited peasantry to confront it. $17

By Any Means Necessary
MALCOLM X

"The imperialists know the only way you will voluntarily turn to the fox is to show you a wolf." In eleven speeches and interviews, Malcolm X presents a revolutionary alternative to this reformist trap, taking up political alliances, women's rights, US intervention in the Congo and Vietnam, capitalism and socialism, and more. $15

The Revolution Betrayed
What Is the Soviet Union and Where Is It Going?
LEON TROTSKY

In 1917 workers and peasants of Russia were the motor force for one of the deepest revolutions in history. Yet within ten years a political counterrevolution by a privileged social layer, whose chief spokesperson was Joseph Stalin, was being consolidated. The classic study of the Soviet workers state and its degeneration. $17. Also in Spanish, Farsi, and Greek.

Lenin's Final Fight
Speeches and Writings, 1922–23
V.I. LENIN

In 1922 and 1923, V.I. Lenin, central leader of the world's first socialist revolution, waged what was to be his last political battle—one that was lost following his death. At stake was whether that revolution, and the international communist movement it led, would remain on the revolutionary proletarian course that brought workers and peasants to power in October 1917. $17. Also in Spanish, Farsi, and Greek.

U.S. Imperialism Has Lost the Cold War
JACK BARNES

The collapse of regimes across Eastern Europe and the USSR claiming to be communist did not mean workers and farmers there had been crushed. In today's sharpening capitalist conflicts and wars, these toilers are joining working people the world over in the class struggle against exploitation. In *New International* no. 11. $14. Also in Spanish, French, Farsi, and Greek.

Capitalism and the Transformation of Africa
Reports from Equatorial Guinea
MARY-ALICE WATERS, MARTÍN KOPPEL

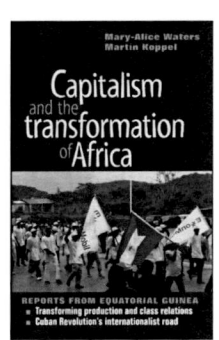

Describes how, as Equatorial Guinea is pulled into the world market, both a capitalist class and a working class are being born. Also documents the work of volunteer Cuban health-care workers there—an expression of the living example of Cuba's socialist revolution. $10. Also in Spanish and Farsi.

The History of the Russian Revolution
LEON TROTSKY

How, under Lenin's leadership, the Bolshevik Party led millions of workers and farmers to overthrow the state power of the landlords and capitalists in 1917 and bring to power a government that advanced their class interests at home and worldwide. Unabridged, 3 vols. in one. Written by one of the central leaders of that socialist revolution. $30. Also in French and Russian.

Maurice Bishop Speaks
The Grenada Revolution and Its Overthrow, 1979–83

The triumph of the 1979 revolution in the Caribbean island of Grenada under the leadership of Maurice Bishop gave hope to millions throughout the Americas. Invaluable lessons from the workers and farmers government destroyed by a Stalinist-led counterrevolution in 1983. $20

Democracy and Revolution
GEORGE NOVACK

The limitations and advances of various forms of democracy in class society, from its roots in ancient Greece through its rise and decline under capitalism. Discusses the emergence of Bonapartism, military dictatorship, and fascism, and how democracy will be advanced under a workers and farmers regime. $17

The Rise and Fall of the Nicaraguan Revolution

Based on ten years of socialist journalism from inside Nicaragua, this special issue of *New International* recounts the achievements and worldwide impact of the 1979 Nicaraguan revolution. It traces the political retreat of the Sandinista National Liberation Front leadership that led to the downfall of the workers and farmers government in the closing years of the 1980s. Documents of the Socialist Workers Party by Jack Barnes, Steve Clark, and Larry Seigle. In *New International* no. 9. $14. Also in Spanish.

The Fight against Fascism in the USA
Forty Years of Struggle Described by Participants
JAMES P. CANNON AND OTHERS

In 1939 some 50,000 people in New York City responded to a call by the Socialist Workers Party to answer a pro-Nazi rally of 20,000. "The question of how to fight fascism was answered in thunderous tones by the magnificent demonstration which raised the cry: Workers Defense Guards to crush the fascist danger!" $5

Lenin's Struggle for a Revolutionary International
Documents, 1907–1916; The Preparatory Years

The debate among revolutionary working-class leaders, including V.I. Lenin and Leon Trotsky, on a socialist response to World War I. $30

Workers and Farmers Governments since the Second World War
ROBERT CHESTER

Articles on the governments that came to power in the revolutions in Yugoslavia, China, Cuba, and Algeria. Such workers and farmers regimes, writes Hansen in his preface, are examples of "the first form of government that can be expected to appear as the result of a successful anticapitalist revolution." $5

WWW.PATHFINDERPRESS.COM

THE CUBAN REVOLUTION AND WORLD POLITICS

From the Escambray to the Congo
In the Whirlwind of the Cuban Revolution
VÍCTOR DREKE

Dreke was second in command of the internationalist column in the Congo led in 1965 by Che Guevara. He recounts the creative joy with which working people have defended their revolutionary course—from Cuba's Escambray mountains to Africa and beyond. $15. Also in Spanish.

Red Zone
Cuba and the Battle against Ebola in West Africa
ENRIQUE UBIETA GÓMEZ

When three African countries were hit in 2014–15 by the Ebola epidemic, Cuba's revolutionary government sent what no other country even pretended to provide: more than 250 volunteer doctors, nurses, and other medical workers. This firsthand account of their actions shows the kind of men and women only a socialist revolution can produce. $17. Also in Spanish and French.

The First and Second Declarations of Havana

Nowhere are the questions of revolutionary strategy that today confront men and women on the front lines of struggles in the Americas addressed with greater truthfulness and clarity than in these uncompromising indictments of imperialist plunder and "the exploitation of man by man." Adopted by million-strong assemblies of the Cuban people in 1960 and 1962. $10. Also in Spanish, French, Farsi, Arabic, and Greek.

Bolivian Diary of Ernesto Che Guevara

Guevara's day-by-day chronicle of the 1966–67 guerrilla campaign in Bolivia, an effort to forge a continent-wide revolutionary movement of workers and peasants and open the road to socialist revolution in South America. $23. Also in Spanish.

Our History Is Still Being Written
The Story of Three Chinese Cuban Generals in the Cuban Revolution
ARMANDO CHOY, GUSTAVO CHUI, MOISÉS SÍO WONG, MARY-ALICE WATERS

"What was the key measure to uproot discrimination against Chinese and blacks in Cuba? It was the socialist revolution itself." New edition sheds light on Chinese Cubans' involvement in Cuba's internationalist course, including in Africa and Latin America. $15. Also in Spanish, French, Farsi, Greek, and Chinese.

Cuba and the Coming American Revolution
JACK BARNES

This is a book about the struggles of working people in the imperialist heartland, the youth attracted to them, and the example set by the Cuban people that revolution is not only necessary—it can be made. It is about the class struggle in the US, where the revolutionary capacities of workers and farmers are today as utterly discounted by the ruling powers as were those of the Cuban toilers. And just as wrongly. $10. Also in Spanish, French, and Farsi.

Cuba and Angola: The War for Freedom
HARRY VILLEGAS ("POMBO")

The story of Cuba's unparalleled contribution to the fight to free Africa from the scourge of apartheid. And how, in the doing, Cuba's socialist revolution was strengthened. $10. Also in Spanish, Farsi, and Greek.

Che Guevara Talks to Young People

Guevara challenges the youth of Cuba and the world to work. To become disciplined. To join the vanguard on the front lines of struggles, small and large. To become a different kind of human being as they fight together with working people of all lands to transform the world. $12. Also in Spanish and Greek.